AN INVITATION INTO
His Chambers

AN INVITATION INTO
His Chambers

The Power of Intimacy with God

VICTORIA CLEVELAND

Printed in the United States of America

ISBN 978-0-9976843-0-8

Developmental Editor: Jamie Calloway Hanauer; www.snsedits.com
Book Cover Design: Audrey Kay Jones; www.audreykjones.com
Interior Book Design: Ghislain Viau; www.creativepublishingdesign.com

To my Father God, my Beloved Jesus,
and Precious Holy Spirit. The beautiful Triune.
Each unique, each perfect, each helping me on this journey
called life. Thank you for chasing me down, apprehending me,
and now…causing me to grow and love you all
more each day. I am blessed beyond measure.

"My desire is that you may come to know, through *personal experience*, the love of Christ which far surpasses mere human knowledge *without* experience. I pray that you may be filled up throughout your whole being with all the fullness of God, *so that* you may have the richest experience of God's presence in your life, completely filled and flooded with God Himself."

(Ephesians 3:19, author's paraphrase)

Table of Contents

Foreword

"THERE'S NEVER BEEN A TIME LIKE THIS"

In this glorious end-time anointing so many wonderful things are happening; the rain and river of the Holy Spirit are flowing. New mantles and assignments as well as prophetic and apostolic power are being released. But most deeply and dearly, there is a call and drawing from the heart of God into the secret place of His presence and love.

This heart call is what "An Invitation into His Chambers" is all about! There is no one I know more qualified and anointed to write and share this intimate call and invitation from God's heart than Vickie Cleveland. She is a seasoned intercessor, a gifted prophetic seer, and a passionate worshipper. Most of all, Vickie is an intimate lover of God. Her overwhelming love and passion for Him, along with her deep revelation and many personal experiences and "God encounters" with dreams and visions, has uniquely prepared and positioned her to write this incredible book of God's heart and love.

The secret place is a very "special place." It's a place for the hungry spiritual heart to experience the overflowing love and the incredible power of intimacy with God. This book is a very "special book"... so get ready to embark on a journey with God that will lead you into the deep intimate places of His heart.

This is your personal "Invitation into His Chambers."

Dr. Jerry Howell, Pastor
Destiny Healing Center

CHAPTER 1

Pillow Talk

Have you ever been in love? When you hear the phrase "pillow talk," what comes to your mind? In the natural realm, the first thing I think of is intimate communication between two people. If you're happily married, this can mean very intimate moments shared between you and your spouse. If you're in love but not yet married, it can mean the intimacy of planning for the future and the promise of things to come. If you've never been in love, don't have a significant other, or don't have a reference point for how "pillow talk" feels and sounds, my prayer is that after completing this book, you will understand and know the reality of intimate communion with God that stems from the foundation of His divine love.

From a spiritual standpoint, what is pillow talk with Jesus? Is it even acceptable? Is it something He desires? The answers to these and other questions will be addressed in the pages of this book. Just as in the natural realm, pillow talk is something very special to be shared with the one you love, so too, it is in the spiritual realm with Jesus. He wants intimate communication with us, His bride. He wants to know our heart, and He wants us to know His. In referencing His bride, I am not describing gender, male or female, but am instead referring to a position of authority. The body of Christ, you and I, male and female, are the bride. He has granted us a high position of authority. This authority will be recognized as we share in intimate communion with Him.

The privilege of intimacy with God is reserved for those who will pursue Him with complete abandonment, and diligently search for His veiled (hidden) truths. The truth that is concealed, or veiled, is not impossible to find, only hidden from the casual seeker.

The Song of Solomon is many times read as an allegory, or a veiled truth. An allegory is simply a representation of a spiritual meaning under the guise or semblance of a natural meaning. This book is an allegory of the bride of Christ, represented by the Shulamite; and her bridegroom King Jesus, represented by Solomon. There are two other books in the Bible sometimes read as allegories; the book of Esther and the book of Ruth.

In Song of Solomon 1:2, the bride speaks to her friends, "Let Him (Jesus the bridegroom) kiss me with the kisses of His mouth." She is declaring she loves Him and wants the intimate touch of His spirit upon her heart. It is obvious she has experienced this "kiss" before, and it has caused her to hunger for more. The kisses of His mouth are the sweet intimacy of His word when it touches her heart in a deep and profound way. This type of intimacy with Jesus can only be found as we put Him first in our heart and lives, spend time with Him, and discover who He really is.

When I first met Jesus in June of 1981, I was at the lowest point of my life and desperate for answers. Not having received love and affirmation as a child, I grew up searching for that love. How many know that God has put an innate sense in all of humankind to love and be loved? I looked for that love and affirmation in many places, but never found it. That is, until I was introduced to Jesus at the age of twenty-eight. I cried out to Him in desperation and experienced His unconditional love in a way that completely overwhelmed me. It was the love I had searched for all my life. At that moment, He completely turned my life upside down (in a wonderful way!) Since that time, I have made Him first in my life and have never regretted a single moment. With Him, there is always more to know and experience, so my journey with Him goes on and on and on …

So let me ask you; when the one you love speaks intimate words of love to you, how do you feel? Does your heart soar? Does your love for them increase? The emotions I'm describing are the same as with the bride of Christ. Because she is in love with her bridegroom Jesus, His words touch the deep recesses of her heart. His words are an intimate kiss that awakens love in her.

Have you been awakened to His love? Song of Solomon 3:5 says there is an appointed time to awaken love. We live in a world full of violence, fear, pain, rejection, and heartache. Never before has there been a time in history when we've needed love to be awakened, as we do now. The love of Jesus will heal every hurt, calm every fear, deliver from every sin, and alleviate every rejection known to man. His love will also empower and cause a tidal wave of restoration and justice to be released into our land.

The invitation to come into His chambers (the secret place) has been sent out. Have you RSVP'd? Are you ready to meet Him in a deeper, more intimate way? Don't wait; the time is now. The Lord is waiting for the one who will pursue Him passionately in the place of intimacy. "… the kingdom of heaven suffers violence, and the violent take it by force." (Matthew 11:12) There is an unrivaled adventure waiting for those who say 'Yes' to His invitation to the secret place. There is a higher place of authority that has not yet been fully discovered but will be revealed and released to those who know their God.

∽✞∾

Prayer and Prophetic Word: My sweet Jesus … lover of my soul, come and touch my innermost being with your words of life. I accept the invitation into your chambers. Awaken my heart to know and love you the way you know and love me. Teach me how to communicate my love to you. Come close, Lord Jesus … as close as you want. I wait on you. I wait in stillness and I am listening. You are a safe Savior. I know you will give me the desires of my heart as I wait on you. But I want to know, Lord … what are your desires? What is in your heart? Just as you long to give me my desires, I long to give you yours. Speak to me Jesus. I am waiting. In your precious name, I pray, amen and amen.

And I hear the Lord saying to us, "Just be with Me, my beloved. You get so busy doing and I want you to just be. Just be with Me. Don't you think I can take care of what you're so busy about? Yes, there are things I would have you do, but most of what you do is of your own making, in your effort to please Me. If you really want to please Me, come away with Me … I am waiting, longing for you."

∽✞∾

Communication through Perfect Love

"There is no fear in love; but perfect love casts out fear, because fear involves torment." (I John 4:18) The definition of perfect love is the love of the Father, Son, and Holy Spirit. There's nothing lacking in it. Consider the communication that goes on between Father God, His Son Jesus, and the Holy Spirit. Do you think they have ever misunderstood one another or withheld their thoughts? No, of course not; they are one spirit and one mind. They know and understand one another completely. They are one in every way. Communication is part of the oneness of perfect love. The Godhead is three in one, moving and communicating in perfect union.

Jesus prayed, "that they all may be one, as you, Father, are in Me, and I in You; that they also may be one in Us …." (John 17:21) What an incredible prayer! Jesus is even now sitting at the right hand of the Father, interceding for us, and the Holy Spirit is showing us the way. As we keep the "communication lines" open to the Holy Spirit, and do not grieve or quench Him, we will continually move toward that 'oneness' with our Father and beloved bridegroom. This is love perfected that has no fear. God wants our communication with the Godhead to be as perfect as it is with Him, His son Jesus Christ and the Holy Spirit. His prayer was for us to move, hear, and speak as one; to have unbroken fellowship with no misunderstandings.

In September of 2005, I was in my prayer room, pressing in for more of the Lord. I was focused totally on Him, longing to see His face and hear His voice, telling Him of my love for Him. Suddenly, I had an open vision, and found myself "transported" into another place and another realm. In this other realm of the spirit, Jesus became liquid love and poured Himself over me. This experience lasted for a while, and when I opened my eyes, it was as if I were seeing my prayer room from afar, as I was still in this other realm. I closed my eyes again and was immediately back in that place with the Lord. As He flooded me with His love, I yielded and received His love, giving my heart back to Him. We were ministering to each other … Him to me and me to Him. When the vision ended, I was completely "drunk" in the spirit. What came to my mind was the phrase, "intoxicated with His love." In that state of being overwhelmed by His love, He took me into intercession, not through prayer but through a dance, and gave me revelation and understanding; my dance of intercession was actually "warfare at the gates." It was incredible and powerful. I also understood that the warfare that night had to be done in a spirit of love; the reason He saturated me with His love before warfare. And I somehow knew it was Him actually warring through me, and it was Him who obtained the victory through it.

That open vision was an example of communication through perfect love and victory through perfect love. In this book, I will share a number of dreams and visions the Lord has given. The purpose of sharing these experiences is to awaken your heart to the reality of what He is speaking to you directly through these visions and to ignite your heart to search for Him in new and deeper ways. There are realms of possibility in Him that we have not yet touched. My prayer is that the place where I stand in intimacy with God will be a launching pad for you who read this and that you will desire to go deeper and higher with Him. I have also included prayers and decrees to help you move forward into all He has determined for you. These prayers and decrees are written in the first person, and should be prayed and decreed aloud by you personally.

ᦗᦗ

Prayer and Declaration: More, Lord, more; I want more of you. Take me to those new places in you and with you. I want the experiences I have with you to cause me to know and ultimately love you more. I want to know what perfect love looks like, feels like, sounds like, and tastes like. I want to be free from fear. Cause me to be one with the Godhead; Father, Son, and Holy Spirit. Lord, I declare that the Godhead, the three-in-one, will become one with me, and will teach me how to communicate with perfect love. I declare as I communicate with perfect love, the kingdom of God will advance in His perfect time and way. In Jesus' name, I pray, amen and amen.

ᦗᦗ

Free To Be Me

Have you ever wanted to do or say something around someone, but knew you would be misunderstood, laughed at, or ridiculed? That's just the way it is many times in human relationships, but not so in our relationship with God. I have discovered I am completely free to be who I really am with Him. I can say what I'm feeling and thinking, release my frustrations and anger to Him, and sometimes cry from the depths of my heart. I can dance, laugh, love, and I can hurt. I know He made me uniquely, and He loves everything about me.

Many times when we hide our emotions around others, we do so because of fear. Fear will shut us down so we cannot express who we really are in God. Have you ever deliberately held back from speaking aloud, such as in a group discussion, because you felt what you had to say would not be accepted? Have you ever wanted to pray with someone, but felt you would be turned down, or criticized? As the body and bride of Christ, we must take off our mask and reveal our identity. Webster's dictionary describes *mask* as "a covering for all or part of the face, worn to conceal one's identity." And if you're wearing a mask, you are masquerading. A *masquerade* is "a false outward show, a facade, or a pretense." As the bride of Christ, we must be transparent with Him and *for* Him. We need to allow Him to be seen in our lives. How can we set people free, and be set free ourselves, if we are not reflecting our true identity? There is freedom in just being who He made you to be.

Sometimes we have to take a risk to reveal who we really are. The book of Esther is the story of a woman in scripture who had to make the choice to take off her mask, very much like we do today. Esther's choice to reveal her true identity led her entire people group into freedom. It was one of the most difficult things she had ever done, but the divine providence of God was guiding and directing her. God had an appointed time for her real identity to come forth, just as He has an appointed time for us. That time is now.

Esther was afraid that revealing who she really was would cost her very life, but her Uncle Mordecai reminded her, "… If you remain completely silent at this time, relief and deliverance will arise for the Jews from another place, but you and your father's house will perish. Yet who knows whether you have come to the kingdom for such a time as this?" (Esther 4:14) Esther had two options to choose from, and she wasn't crazy about either one. Would she risk revealing her true Jewish heritage to save her people, or would she remain silent, and have everyone she loved destroyed, for the sake of saving herself? She felt the weight of her decision. She had not been called by her husband the king for thirty days, and felt she had lost favor with him. She also knew she would be put to death if she came into the king's presence without being summoned. The situation called for desperate measures, so she decided to fast and pray for three days, along with her maids, saying, "and so I will go to the king, which is against the law, and if I perish, I perish!" (Esther 4:16) But she had a God-given plan.

She invited the king to a banquet of wine, which was a replay of their engagement night. She had to be sure of his love for her before she made her request. She also made a seemingly odd request by inviting Haman, her enemy, as well. At the end of the banquet, still not completely convinced the timing was right, she invited the king to a second banquet of wine, along with Haman. Feeling the timing was right on the second night, and at the king's plea to know what was in her heart, she said, "If I have found favor in your sight, O king, and if it pleases the king, let my life be given me at my petition, and my people at my request. For we have been sold, my people and I, to be destroyed, to be killed, and to be annihilated." (Esther 7:3-4) Esther chose at that moment to take off her mask and reveal her true identity. She knew what was at risk, but she also knew the king loved her and the timing was right. And it paid off.

The king was furious that someone would want to harm his queen, and asked, "Who is he, and where is he, who would dare presume in his heart to do such a thing?" And Esther said, "The adversary and enemy is this wicked Haman!" (Esther 7:5-6) At that moment, Esther's enemy became the king's enemy, and Haman hung on his own gallows before the day ended.

In the days of the Persian Empire, any decree made by a king could not be revoked or changed. But convinced of the king's love for her, Esther took it a step further and asked for another decree to be written so that the Jews would be able to protect themselves from the original decree that called for their annihilation. All of this happened because Esther chose to "take off her mask" and reveal her true identity. There is power in revealing who you really are!

There is also another powerful truth in this story that often goes unnoticed. In the story Esther continues, "Had we been sold as male and female slaves, I would have held my tongue, although the enemy could never compensate for the king's loss." (7:4) Esther was aware the king would lose something very precious to him if she did not speak up. She came to understand her value to the king. Esther was compelled by the Holy Spirit to speak up because the enemy was out to kill, steal, and destroy her and her people. Sound familiar? In the spiritual realm, this is exactly what the enemy wants to do to God's people. But we must be willing to take off our mask and reveal our true identity. In doing so, we will reveal the reality of His love for us, as well as the deception of the enemy. There is power in revealed truth.

For us to walk in pretense concerning who we really are would not only allow the enemy to steal something very valuable from us, but also to those around us; most of all, it would be a great loss to our bridegroom King. He has a bride that He is waiting and longing for, to reveal His glory through. It would be a great loss to Him if we never stepped into the full purpose and destiny He intended.

Our full destiny is not just in eternity but in the here and now. The Lord wants us to live in freedom from oppression, bondage, sickness, and every form of harassment the enemy will try to bring. If we don't break free, take off our mask, and choose to live in the fullness of our purpose and calling, then the exorbitant price He paid for our freedom here on earth is wasted. Living in our true identity is the only proper response to the extravagant price He paid. Not only is it the proper response, but it is the only one that will allow us to fully enjoy our journey.

❦

Prayer and Declaration: Lord, I confess and repent because there are areas of my life in which I am wearing a mask to protect myself. I confess that the fear of what others may think of me has caused me to hide who I really am, and not be transparent. It has caused a wall of separation between me and others. But more than that, Lord, I have not understood the value you place on me, and all that you paid for. I want to be free to be myself. Now, Lord, make me fully alive because I know who I am in you. Let me live in the confidence of being who you made me to be. It is only then that I will grow and mature into the bride I am destined to become. Lord, I declare I will not believe the lies of the enemy any longer, and he will not hold me back from being who you made me to be. I declare I am the righteousness of God in Christ, and you love me completely just the way I am. I decree I am not ashamed to be who you have made me to be. And I declare I will walk in the fullness of all that you paid to redeem me, completely understanding the high value you place on me. Thank you, Lord! In your precious name, I pray, amen and amen.

෧෦෨

In the Secret Place

Where is the place we can freely have "pillow talk?" Where can we be free to just be who we really are, to express ourselves to God in a deep way without fear of rejection? It may be your prayer closet, a bedroom, or a corner of your house; wherever you can be alone with God without interruption. It is an experiential place. It is in this place He will wait, look, and yearn for you. He already knows everything about you, so there's nothing you can tell him that would surprise or shock Him. But He wants your heart wide open to Him. He wants to hear your voice and see your face. "O my dove, in the clefts of the rock, in the secret places of the cliff, let me see your face, let me hear your voice; for your voice is sweet, and your face is lovely." (Song of Solomon 2:14)

He refers to us as His dove because a dove does not have peripheral vision; they can only see straight ahead. They have single vision, which is what the Lord sees in us as well. He sees our eyes are for Him alone. We may be at a place in our life where that reality has not fully manifested, but when God looks at us, He sees the finished product. He sees the bride who has made herself ready. And that is how He relates to us, from what He knows to be true.

He wants us to hide in Him, *THE* rock. We can hide in the wounds (clefts) of Jesus (the rock). We do this by having our eyes, our mind, and our heart fixed on Him. When the storms of life come, there is a guaranteed safe place: it is in Him. The storms may knock us off of our focus temporarily, but the key is to get our attention back to Him quickly. He has the answers to whatever we may be facing in the storm. "The name of the Lord is a strong tower, the righteous run to it and are safe." (Proverbs 18:10)

What does it mean to be in the secret places of the cliff? A secret place is a place hidden in God, away from the world. It is there we find safety. While we are climbing the mountain of life, the Lord provides places hewn out of the rock that we can enter into, where we can rest and be refreshed. There are places in our journey He has ordained to meet with us and show us things. But there is also something He desires from us in the secret place. He says, "Let me see your face, let me hear your voice; for your voice is sweet, and your face is lovely." (Song of Solomon 2:14) Have you ever considered that God longs to see your face and hear your voice? Beloved, He is so enamored with you. He is crazy in love with you. He loves the way you look and your voice is sweet to Him. How good is that!

"He who dwells in the secret place of the Most High shall abide under the shadow of the Almighty." (Psalm 91:1) What does it mean to dwell in the secret place? To dwell or linger is to stay *indefinitely*: to abide. *Abide* means "to stay, live, dwell, and take up permanent residence." Abiding refers not only to a physical place, but also to an attitude or a condition of the heart. As you mature and grow in intimacy with the Lord, there comes a time that even when you leave your designated secret place, your *heart* is still there no matter where you go. You may be running errands, picking up kids, or getting ready for a business meeting, but you are still communing with God as you go about your busy day. Even though your mind may not be focused on God, your heart and spirit are constantly communing with Him. When you experience involuntary prayers springing up from within without even thinking about them, then you have reached a place of constant communion.

Abiding under the shadow of the Almighty is living constantly under the shadow of His protection, His wing. Where there is a shadow, there is also light (from the Son). His shadow is a place of safety and security. Do you feel safe and secure? If not, move under His shadow of comfort and protection. It's called the secret place. Again, it is a condition of your heart and mind, although it can be a physical place as well.

Sometimes He will call us to come away with Him into the secret place at very inopportune times, but it is a test. Will we come when we hear Him calling? Will we lay aside our agenda and come? There are times when He calls me that I am very busy with my own agenda, but all He really wants is a couple of minutes of my time to get me refocused on Him. What a sweet place of rest. When I refocus, my mind is cleared and I can put things in perspective. Refocusing helps me get my priorities back in order. I've also had times I just can't figure out the best way to do a certain task, but as I stop and wait on Him, and ask for help, He gives me the wisdom I need.

The Holy Spirit has taught me that coming quickly when He calls is a place of foundational obedience. Will you come when you hear Him calling? Will you lay aside your immediate agenda and come? It is important to Him because He knows what you need more than you do, and that is why He is calling you to come at inopportune times. He desires to bless you as you are obedient to come quickly.

⚬❦⚬

Prayer and Declaration: Lord, I pray like David did that you would hide me in the secret place of your presence, away from the tongues of men. Let me find you in that sweet place of communion, and as I wait, let me hear and know your heart in a deeper way. Thank you for the secret place. It is so precious to me. I pray to always be drawn there to meet with you. And Lord, I want to dwell in that secret place as I go about my day. I pray for my spirit to be in constant communion with you. I don't want to be separated from you, My Lord and Master and Lover of my soul; I want to be constantly under the shadow of your wings. I long for an unbroken communion of my spirit with yours. Lord, I declare that I will train my eyes to see and acknowledge you first in everything. I decree the secret place will be my first priority from this point forward, as you have taught me the importance you place on it. And I decree Lord, that out of that time will come the revelation, wisdom, and power I need for the day. In Jesus' name, I pray, amen and amen.

ॐ

The Atmosphere of Intimacy

In the natural realm, you set the mood for "pillow talk." You put on some soft music, turn the lights down low, and maybe have a fragrant candle burning in the room. It is the same in the spiritual realm. To set the mood for this exchange of love between your spirit and His, you may want to put on some soft worship or soaking music and have the lights dimmed; this is an intimate time. In the secret place, you quiet your heart, turn all your thoughts and attention to the Lord, and begin to look for His presence. You speak words of love and adoration to Him. Your words will cause Him to draw near. As you open your heart to Him, He opens His heart to you. "The king has brought me into his chambers." (Song of Solomon 1:4) What are His chambers? They are

rooms or private places away from the noise and busyness
of the house. It can be your bedroom, an adjoining sitting
room, or possibly your designated prayer room. His chambers
are the most private places. Places of quiet and solitude are
the most appropriate for pillow talk. Sometimes the Lord
will call us into His chamber to be with Him for no other
reason than He wants to spend time with us. Have you
ever felt that drawing? It's real. He wants your undivided
attention, your focus. It is in His chamber, His secret place,
that He will reveal the secrets of His heart. And it is there
in His chamber that He will tenderize and heal your heart
in deep ways.

Whether you realize it or not, there is an atmosphere of
heaven in the secret place. The secret place is the place where
heaven and earth meet and kiss. It is the place where His glory
"tabernacles" with us. When you come to the place where
you and God are to meet, there is an atmosphere created
just by your expectation. Webster's dictionary describes
atmosphere as "air, ambience, climate, environment, feeling,
impression." The atmosphere you create by your expectations
will facilitate your time of intimacy with the Lord. This
intimacy is a most precious and holy exchange. Because He
is a holy God, everything He releases to you will be holy. It
will be beyond anything you can experience in the natural
sense of intimacy, because it comes from the One who
created everything, including us. He is altogether pure, and

what He gives is pure. There have been many times I have experienced the exchange of pure and holy intimacy with Him that is far beyond what I know in the natural realm.

As you go further and deeper with the Lord, you will experience the atmosphere of intimacy extend beyond the designated secret place. There have been many times just driving in my car, as I turn my heart and mind towards Him, that the very atmosphere in the car changes, and I can tangibly feel Him. In those moments, I worship. I worship the One who has come into my midst and honored me with His presence. I worship the one whom I love with all my heart, and who loves me. My worship is a spiritual embrace. And He reciprocates with His embrace of love.

Do you know you can change the atmosphere wherever you go? As you choose to take Him with you, abide in Him and allow Him to abide in you, the atmosphere of heaven is released wherever you go, and into whatever you do. This is known as "hosting His presence." There are not many that will host His presence, but that is what He longs for. Will you be one that changes the atmosphere wherever you go?

There is another benefit of hosting His presence. As you release the atmosphere of His very "essence" wherever you go, it will draw the hearts of those who need Him. This is called "presence evangelism." You never have to speak a word or do anything. As you become a portal of entry for heaven to invade the earth realm, the supernatural will be released into the atmosphere around you. This was a common occurrence to some of the great men of old, such as Charles Finney, whose presence evangelism caused people in a cotton mill to fall to their knees in repentance. This presence evangelism accompanied men like Jonathan Edwards and George Wakefield who stood without speaking a word, and thousands understood their need for a savior, felt God's love; and cried out for Him. These great men of faith walked as one with God, releasing His presence and love into the atmosphere. They walked in intimacy with the Lord that many have not experienced. Do you want it? Are you willing to host His presence?

☙

Prayer and Declaration: Lord, I understand the importance you place on intimacy and the atmosphere of intimacy. Lord, I am asking for an anointing to draw you. I want to know and feel your presence when you enter our secret place. I want you to be pleased when I drop everything and come immediately when you call, and I want you to be delighted when you find me waiting for you, elated that I have prepared for our time together. Lord, you are my bridegroom, and my desire is to please you. I want to abide in you and allow you to abide in me. I want to become familiar with your atmosphere of holy intimacy, not only in our secret place but wherever I go. I declare, Lord, that I will be a portal for heaven to come down and kiss the earth. I declare I will be a conduit of your love to a dying world; a world that is searching for a love that only you can give. Take away anything in me, Lord, that hinders intimacy with you, and I declare I will give you all the glory. In your precious name, I pray, amen and amen.

❧

What's in a Whisper?

When you whisper, your words are meant only for the person close enough to hear them. To whisper means to talk softly and privately, to speak using the breath and not the vocal cords. Whispers are private. They are not for everyone to hear. Sometimes they are secrets. Frequently they are intimate. In the context of love, a whisper carries a deeper expression of intimacy than what a normal conversation carries.

In his teaching on "*Bridal Intercession,*" Gary Wiens said, "The most powerful human voice in my life is the softly whispered words of my wife on the pillow at night, because we are a people in love." Listen, love is powerful. It never fails. A whisper is a powerful form of communication in the context of love! It ignites the heart in a way nothing else can. A whisper will cause you to tune your ear to the one speaking, especially if the one speaking is the one you're in love with. A whisper can draw two hearts together and join them as one.

Have you ever heard the Lord whisper your name? His whisper is a still small voice. Has He ever whispered a secret to you? If He has, then you know the power of that whisper. When you are in tune with Jesus and are aware of His presence, the whispers come more often and are more meaningful. Jesus wants to share His heart with you same as you want to share your heart with the one you love. Our mind, will, and emotions can be revealed in a whisper and powerfully move the one that hears. Have you whispered His name today? Have you drawn Him by the breath of your words? You can, you know. He died to make you His. Now He waits for your affections to be first and foremost His. Whisper His name. There is power in that whisper.

❧

Prayer and Declaration: Lord, would you whisper the secrets of your heart to me? I want to know those things that are near and dear to your heart. The secrets you don't share with just anyone. I want to know those secrets, Jesus. I care about how you feel. It's important to me. You are my beloved Bridegroom, my inheritance. Let your breath be like a sweet caress upon my face. Let the words you whisper draw us closer together. Make us one, sweet Jesus. Make us one. Lord, I declare that my whisper, the deep things I share with you, will be like a sweet kiss to you. Let it be sweet Lord, and touch your heart in a deeply meaningful way. Lord, I declare that my whisper will ignite your heart. I declare that our gently whispered words will carry the power of love that will change hearts and lives wherever we go. In your precious name, I pray, amen and amen.

☙

The Romantic of All the Ages

I was in an evening prayer and soaking session at my home church and the worship leader was gently playing the keyboard. As the vision began, I found myself in a large meadow, with lush, green rolling hills and enormous trees. Across from the meadow were fields of beautiful wildflowers, all colors and varieties. I was in a small clearing atop one of the hills, lying on my back with my hands tucked behind my head and my ankles crossed. I was completely relaxed and serene, enjoying the beauty around me. I felt the gentle warmth of the sun's rays on my face and a slight breeze, causing the leaves to rustle on the nearby trees. As I looked out across the meadow, I saw the Lord nearby in the field of wildflowers. He appeared to be very busy and the look on His face showed joy and contentment. He would bend down and pluck a flower, and then glance over at me and smile. When He picked the flower, I would smell it from where I lay. He seemed to be looking for specific flowers, examining and making a careful selection of the ones He wanted. Each time He would choose and pluck a flower, He would glance my way and smile. I would smell the fragrance of the flower He chose. Each one was unique and smelled wonderful. He did this repeatedly, and each time He would glance my way with a flower in hand, I would smell the scent from where I lay.

He did this over and over, and when He had gathered a huge bouquet, He began to run to me, smiling and laughing in a way I had never seen before. He was a little breathless by the time He got to me. Then He bent down and laid the huge bouquet on my stomach, all the while smiling and laughing. Then, with a gleam in His eye, He said, "These (referring to the flowers) are in *our* garden!" The aroma of the flowers was intoxicating and almost overwhelming in a sweet, delightful way. The fragrance, plus the understanding of what the Lord was saying to me at that moment, touched my heart deeply and profoundly. Then my vision ended.

Jesus is the true romantic. Ladies and gentlemen, in the natural realm, we all want to be romanced. Don't we want to know there is someone out there who finds us irresistible? Someone who will take the time and effort to show us how important we are to them? Don't we want to know there is someone who really cares about the way we feel, and what's important to us? Moreover, that they care, and go through the effort to show us and make us feel it. I tell you, that is exactly what Jesus will do, and will continue to do if we will take the time to come away with Him. Love takes time. Love requires being vulnerable and opening up to the one you love. Sharing the deepest emotions of your heart is romance at its best.

When you're in love, romance comes naturally. It is not "faked" or forced. It is a very real emotion of the heart. Jesus loves us so much that He died for us. We were on His mind during the week of His crucifixion. Hebrews 12:2b says, "… for the joy that was set before Him, He endured the cross, despising the shame, and has sat down at the right hand of the throne of God." What was Jesus thinking as He went down that hill into Jerusalem for the last time? Beloved, He was looking ahead to the time when we would be presented to Him by the Father, a pure and spotless bride. He set His face like flint because He was going after us. Just the thought of us caused His heart to race wildly. He knew the price He had to pay was not too great. It was worth it. We were worth it. We had won His heart.

In Song of Solomon 6:4, our bridegroom says, "O my love, you are as beautiful as Tirzah, lovely as Jerusalem, awesome as an army with banners!" This verse gives us a glimpse of the depth of His love and passion for us. He calls us His love. That's pretty romantic. Then He calls us beautiful and lovely. That makes us feel good. Then He says we are awesome. We are really feeling good about ourselves now. Then He makes a declaration that just blows my mind. In verse 5b, He says, "Turn your eyes away from me, for they have overcome me!" Can you imagine? Here is our great bridegroom King, the one who holds the universe in His hands, speaks things into existence with the breath of His mouth, and subdues all the nations. Nevertheless, He is captured by one glance from our eyes: just one glance. He is hopelessly in love with us! Just one look into our eyes will overcome and overwhelm Him. Are you getting the picture? Do you understand the effect a lovesick bride will have on her bridegroom? Just the thought of it causes my heart to soar. And listen, this love, this romance, is unlike any earthly romance. It is higher and deeper. It comes from the depths of the One who created us and knows everything about us. It is born and consummated in purity and holiness.

A love that is consummated in purity will burn brightly with the fire of holy passion and devotion. "… [Loves] flames are flames of fire, a most vehement flame. Many waters cannot quench love, nor can the floods drown it." (Song of Solomon 8:6-7) Just as the bridegroom's love will overcome all, so the passion of the bride for her bridegroom will overcome all in the last days. There is nothing thrown at us that can put out the fire of love once we have been romanced by the King of Kings. His love is greater than any adversity or challenge we may face.

Jesus, our bridegroom, is the absolute romantic of all the ages. Think about it … He made Himself of no reputation, taking on the form of man, to come and rescue us, so we could live in eternity with Him. Our beautiful bridegroom King disguised Himself as a mere man to come and win us back to Himself. He has drawn us to Himself by Holy Spirit.

He has said, "This one is Mine!" He's given us an engagement ring in the form of Holy Spirit, to sustain us and remind us of His imminent return. And when He comes for us, it will be in all His glory and splendor! The beauty and majesty of who He is will astound us.

᠅

Prayer and Declaration: My precious bridegroom Jesus, come and romance my heart. I need to know how you feel about me. Father God has created me with this intrinsic desire to be loved completely, with the intent that you, Lord, will be the one to completely fulfill that desire. I say yes to you, Jesus. I open my heart wide and allow you to come in and speak your words of love over me. And Holy Spirit, give me the words to romance my King. Let my words be sweet to Him. Let them draw His heart and fulfill His heart. How incredible to know the King of Kings, the lover of my soul, is also the romantic of all the ages, and His heart is towards me. I decree that every obstacle that is standing in the way of our being one will be removed by Him, and I decree our oneness will cause many to hunger for the same. In His precious name, I pray, amen and amen.

᠅

Love Letters

Have you ever received a love letter from someone? How did it make you feel? If you loved that someone, I'm sure it made you feel special. Have you ever written a love letter to the one you love? While writing, your heart was wide open and your emotions flowing, right? Love letters can be a powerful form of communication. Not only do they reveal the heart of the one writing, but seeing the words on paper will cause a deeper revelation and "setting in" of those words into your spirit. One of my intents in writing this book is to cause you to realize and experience deeper communication with God through every means possible. Writing is one form of communication that involves a combination of your senses.

In May of 2005, I was at a Soaking Prayer Center in Toronto, and during one of the training sessions, the instructor had us quiet ourselves before the Lord, spend some time just listening to Him, and then write down what we were hearing. Our instructions were not to think about what we were writing, but as the Lord gave a verse or a specific thought, to flow with it, and continue writing until the anointing lifted. I was surprised and delighted by what the Lord spoke during that time, and have held this love letter close to my heart since then. It has been a source of strength and encouragement in some very difficult times. I pray as you read it, you would take it as a love letter directly to you from the Lord, as I did, because it is not just for me, but it is for His bride, of which you are one.

The Lord said, *"My child, I've always loved you. You've always looked for love in others, but they haven't fulfilled your need as I can. Don't look for others to fulfill that need for love. I put that need deep in you, and I'm the only one that can completely fulfill it. I am your Father. I am your beloved bridegroom. I am the one you are searching for. It is Me. Look not to another to meet that need.*

Listen for My words of love to you. Do not look for words from others. They will not satisfy. Only the words I speak to you will satisfy. Only my touch will meet that need in you. Only my touch will meet your need. Only my eyes will cause your heart to soar. I have dove's eyes for you. Come to me, and let me pour my love balm over you. There is no other love that can compare to mine. So look up higher. Look to me. I am yours and you are mine. You are my beloved." Selah. (This Hebrew word means to pause, and think about what has just been said.)

Take time to share your deepest feelings with the Lord in the form of a letter. Make it simple, childlike, and real. There is something deep within each of us that desires an open, honest relationship with our beloved. Go for it. Don't be afraid to open your heart in a way you never have. He is a safe Savior; He will never hurt you. He is trustworthy and will hold your heart in a way no one else can or ever will. I know because He has held mine for many years.

After you have opened up your heart and shared with the Lord, then allow Him to pour out His thoughts and feelings to you in the same way. He longs for you to know how He feels about you. Remember, love takes time. Give Him the time He desires. You won't regret one minute of it.

༜

Prayer and Declaration: Lord, your feelings are important to me. I want to know what makes you happy and what saddens your heart. I want to know all about you. Would you reveal your deepest thoughts to me? Would you express your feelings to me as I wait before you with pen and paper in hand? I want to be a conduit of your Spirit and flow with your emotions. I want to be an extension of your very Spirit. And Lord, teach me how to put my thoughts and feelings for you on paper. I know you would love to get a love letter from your bride. Teach me how to express my feelings to you in a deeper way. Lord, I decree I will begin to communicate with you in ways I never have. I decree, Lord, that my communication with you will take on a new dimension, and I will begin to learn all the different ways you have created for me to touch and speak to you. And Lord, I decree as you teach me, I will share and teach others the same. In Jesus' name, I pray, amen and amen.

༜

Beauty Treatments
(For Women Only)

Don't we want to be beautiful in the eyes of the one we love? And what great lengths we go to in order to look our best. The clothes, the hair, the makeup; they are all part of it. Deep down, we have a need for approval from the one we love. Think about this in the spiritual realm. How do we make ourselves attractive to God? It is by His Spirit. The Holy Spirit gives beauty preparations. "Now the young woman pleased him, and she obtained his favor; so he readily gave beauty preparations to her, besides [more than] her allowance." (Esther 2:9) If we will yield to the Holy Spirit's work in our hearts, He will give us beauty treatments that we can't get anywhere else. These treatments are not available to just anyone. They cannot be purchased at your local cosmetics counter, or bought at the best salon in town. The result of these beauty treatments given by the Holy Spirit can be seen by all we meet. They are desired by all, but only the bride of Christ has the privilege to receive them. What are these beauty treatments?

One is the "clothes" we wear. The Holy Spirit resting on us is beautiful to the Lord and to others. Put Him on, abide in Him and let Him abide in you. A tender yielded spirit is evidence of the Holy Spirit resting on you. There is something very beautiful about a woman who walks with grace and dignity, knowing who she is in Him. It makes a statement to the world. Women who know who they are do not have to prove anything to the world. They are not out to impress the world in any way. Their inner beauty is revealed to those around them and is unlike anything the world has seen. Not only will people be drawn to their inner beauty, but there will be a fragrance surrounding them that will have a powerful attraction, both to believers and unbelievers.

Another beauty secret is our hair. That signifies our covering. He alone is our covering of glory. Allow Him not only to be your covering but also to be the one whom all your decisions stem from. That does not mean becoming subservient, but it means having the same agenda as He does. Realize His ways and wisdom is far beyond ours. Understand His plans, His highest and best for us are custom made. Sometimes it takes a high level of trust on our part to submit to Him. But as we allow Him to be our covering, the places He leads us and the adventures we have in Him will be beyond what we could know or experience otherwise.

Several years ago I was invited to a friends' CD launching party. Headed that way, I was feeling a little down because I didn't have someone beside me, and feeling a little uncomfortable at the thought of going alone. As I was driving, the Lord spoke and said, *"I will be your escort."* I can't tell you what that meant to me. Those five little words changed my whole outlook. I had a great time that evening because I knew I was covered. My feelings of being vulnerable and insecure were gone. I felt a confidence that had not been there previously. When I got home, I looked up the word *escort*. Webster's dictionary defines it as "One who accompanies to give protection and show honor." That is exactly what He did. Do you need an escort? If you are covered by Him,

He is with you to give protection and show honor. You can move with confidence because you have the most incredible escort of all time!

One last beauty secret is our makeup. Unlike traditional makeup, it represents being transparent to all who look at you so they can see Him. A few months ago, I was a little paranoid about turning another year older, and since I am not the type to grow old gracefully, I decided to have my first chemical peel. A couple of days after the treatment, I began to peel. I was looking in the mirror and helping the process along by pulling off the flaking skin, when I heard the Lord say, *"Take the mask off."* After pondering that for a while, I understood He was referring to something much more profound than my face peeling.

A mask is a covering of all or part of the face, worn to conceal one's identity. If you have a mask on, you are masquerading. That is a false outward show; a facade or a pretense. We are in a time when we must take off our mask and reveal our true identity. Fear will often keep us from revealing our true identity. "For God has not given us a spirit of fear, but of power and love and of a sound mind." (2 Timothy 1:7) Confront the spirit of fear and move forward into your destiny. That is what Esther did when, in a time of dire circumstances, she knew she could no longer hide her true identity. To do so would mean the death of her and her people. She overcame her fear and revealed her true identity to the king, and her enemy became the king's enemy.

As the bride of Christ, we have an identity that will shatter the darkness in this world, and cause the kingdoms of this world to become the kingdoms of our God. This is our privilege as His bride and partner. Revealing Him in our transparency is a strategic key in this hour. It is what we are created for. It is one of our most coveted beauty secrets.

In summary, how would you like to have beauty treatments and special beauty secrets that not only save you time and money, but also have a 100% money back guarantee? His Word, which is truth, says, "… He renews our youth like the eagles." (Psalm 103:5) That alone would save us all a lot of time and money in our search for renewed youth! In addition, another result of the beauty secrets that Holy Spirit gives is found in Esther 2:15b: "Esther obtained favor in the sight of all who saw her." Would you like to have the favor of all who see you? In the Song of Solomon, the Lord says His bride is the most beautiful among women. He states this three times in Song of Solomon, and praises her beauty, letting her know she is the MOST beautiful one in His eyes. Don't we want to be the most beautiful one to the one we are in love with? Let me just say here that even though this section is specifically for women, men can partake of these beauty preparations as well. Because we are all the bride of Christ, men and women alike, the Holy Spirit will adorn us all.

Let's take one last look in the book of Esther, and insert ourselves into the story line, as it would pertain to us in the present day. Esther represents the bride of Christ, Hegai represents the Holy Spirit, and the king represents Jesus our bridegroom King. In 2:8-18, we see Esther (the bride of Christ) taken to the king's palace and finding favor with Hegai (the Holy Spirit). He gave her over and above her share of beauty preparations, so much so, that the king (our bridegroom King Jesus) could not help but choose her. One of the things I find interesting is she chose only what was recommended by the Holy Spirit when the time came to go in to the king. For a year, she prepared for that one night with the king. She filled her mind and heart with only him. She wanted to look the way that would please him, speak only what would please Him, and act to please Him. The fact that her heart was pure and undivided towards him was very attractive to the king.

How do we measure up to that example? I believe the standard of the world sometimes gets in the way of our pleasing Him first. We are inundated with the way we should look, act and think by the standard of the world. God's ways are so much higher than ours, and His thoughts so much higher than ours. God desires purity, which has a two-fold blessing. One, He says the pure in heart shall see Him. In addition, as we behold Him, we cannot help but become more like Him. And guess what girls ... the more we see Him, the more we fall in love with Him; far above anyone or anything else we could desire.

❧

Prayer and Declaration: Holy Spirit, I ask for beauty preparations that would please my beloved bridegroom, King Jesus. I pray, Jesus, for the anointing to draw you by what the Holy Spirit has released to me. I want with all of my heart to please you above all others. I want your heart to soar when you look at me. Anoint me, Holy Spirit, with grace and inward beauty. Let my inward beauty be revealed outwardly, and draw others to you as well. Let me release a fragrance that will draw others to you, and let grace be a powerful testimony of your work in my life. Let my inward strength be revealed outwardly in the form of boldness. Let my secret life in you be revealed by an outward release of power to those who need it. Lord, I declare from this day forward, I will seek after those attributes that are pleasing to you. I understand, Lord, and declare to be yielded to the Holy Spirit in this area, and recognize the beauty preparations He gives are so much more desirable than what the world has to offer. I declare, Lord, to be a bride that lives for you, first and foremost. In Jesus' name, I pray, amen and amen.

❧

Reflections on Chapter One

1. List some of the ways you can engage in more meaningful communication with God.

2. How have you been hiding your true identity, and in what ways can you reveal it more fully?

3. Write at least three ways you plan to commit yourself more fully to God.

_____

_____

_____

_____

_____

_____

_____

_____

_____

CHAPTER 2

Fundamentals of Communication

Communication—In the natural realm, it is *absolutely* the biggest problem in all of history. It has been the number one cause of heartbreak, disappointment, discouragement, separation and divorce. It has been the culprit of misunderstandings, broken friendships, and business deals gone wrong, just to name a few. Ninety percent of all problems begin with communication. However, if used effectively the way God intended, it can be the greatest weapon we possess. I refer to it as a weapon because if used the right way, it can thwart the enemy's plan, release power, and advance the kingdom of God.

I was on a plane bound for the International House of Prayer in Kansas City last week, and when the plane touched down, everyone immediately reached for his or her cell phone to check for messages. It was a simultaneous action by everyone on the plane, including me. We all have an innate desire to be connected to others, to be in touch with those we love. Because we are made in God's image, we know He has the same desire. He wants to be connected with those He loves. When we don't take time for Him, it grieves His heart.

If we can grasp a few simple fundamental truths regarding communication with the Lord, and use them not only in our time with Him, but in human relationships, we can experience victory in an area that can be very challenging.

❧

Prayer and Declaration: Thank you, Lord, that you have created me in your image, and you want to be in communication with me at all times. Forgive me for the times I have been too busy or too distracted to communicate with you, verbally or silently. Lord, you have the answers to every question, and if I would just realize this and take the time to find out what your solution is, I know I could navigate the storms of life with much more ease. Father, I declare I will begin to seek you for the answers I need, and will purposefully inquire of you concerning all that troubles me. I declare my ears will be open and my mind fixed on the solution you are releasing at any given moment. I declare I will walk in wisdom and understanding of your ways. In Jesus' name, I pray, amen and amen.

Love Never Fails

Keep this uppermost in your mind; write it on your heart, live it, breathe it, and experience it. Love never fails. It is a basic principle on the spiritual and natural level. Liken it unto the law of gravity. You can count on it. For the sake of my subject, I am going to discuss the *spiritual* aspect of this love as it pertains to us. As we walk in love, our communication will become what God intended.

First, we know we love Him because He first loved us. Think about that for a moment. Even on our darkest day, He loves us unconditionally. There is no sin, no disappointment, and no mistake so big that His love cannot prevail over it. His love prevails over everything. "Many waters [the waters of trial] cannot quench love, nor can the floods drown it." (Song of Solomon 8:7) What an incredible promise. His love toward us never fails. We are forever changed by His love, and His love grows stronger and deeper with time. We can never experience all of it because there is always more. There is always more with Spirit to spirit communication, too. He will always have more to speak to you concerning His love and His ways, and the Holy Spirit will always give you more to say to Him. It is ongoing and never ending.

Because love never fails, we can rest assured that if we continually release His love to another by our words or actions, the desired result will be accomplished. It may take a while, but His word is true. Love never fails. Sometimes people who have been hurt and wounded create walls around themselves to keep from being hurt again. In these cases, love may take longer to break through the walls; but be assured every time you speak and act in love a piece of the wall is chipped away.

Let's review from His word what love looks like that never fails. "Love suffers long and is kind; love does not envy; love does not parade itself, is not puffed up; does not behave rudely, does not seek its own, is not provoked, thinks no evil; does not rejoice in iniquity, but rejoices in the truth; bears all things, believes all things, hopes all things, endures all things." (1 Cor. 13:4-7) Paul said love is the more excellent way. Prior to these verses, He was speaking about spiritual gifts that edify and lift up the body. He spoke about the value and diversity of these gifts, but acknowledged without love, the gifts profit nothing. Love is the substance that gives meaning to all of the spiritual gifts. Love is the earmark of authenticity and the stamp of God's approval. Love is the key that will validate whatever is done in the name of Jesus.

The Hearing Heart

Listen not just with your ears, but listen with your heart. This type of listening will take us beyond the natural realm and cause us to understand and know things that we would not ordinarily be able to know. Then, out of that understanding, we will be able to respond in a way that will cause love to escalate. The Lord wants us to listen with our heart because this is how He listens. It takes practice to be able to listen with your heart. The more you practice, the better you will be able to discern quickly what He is saying at any given moment or situation. The secrets of the Lord are with those who fear Him, and part of that reverential fear and awe involves listening intently to what He has to say. Many times, He will "drop" something into our spirit, and we hear what He says because we are in tune to Him. Have you ever leaned into, or pressed in, to hear what He is saying? If you haven't, try it. You won't be disappointed.

The enemy will sometimes try to convince you that you don't hear Him speaking; it was just your own thoughts. Ask the Lord to reveal the spirit of truth in what you hear, and He will. What He speaks will never contradict His written word, although His spoken word will many times not be found specifically in the written word. Nevertheless, it will never contradict His character. His spoken word will always be motivated by His love. His word, His character, and His love are a sure plumb line you can measure your hearing by. As you train yourself to listen with your heart or your spirit, you will know when you're hearing His voice, or if it's another. Get into His presence and hear His voice. In time, your communication with Him will be a constant flow.

The following is a love letter the Lord wrote me during a very critical time in my life. I was at a major crossroad and desperate for direction. I needed to hear from Him. I postured myself quietly before Him with pen and paper and waited. I leaned in to let Him know I expected to hear from Him. He didn't disappoint. Once more, I want to reiterate; that every vision, dream, and letter the Lord has given me, is not just for me alone, but for the entire body of Christ. It is for you, the one reading this. Let the following speak to you personally in a deep way. Listen with your heart for the voice of the Lord speaking directly to you.

"My beloved, how can I tell you how much I love you? You've given your time, your love, your heart and your desires. I see your sacrifices, and I love you for that. How can I tell you all that is in my heart for you? There is so much I want to give you, so much I want to tell you. There are many things that I have yet to speak, to show, and to reveal. My heart is full. The things you're not sure of; the things you wonder about; be patient, my love, the time will come. Be patient – did I not tell you I would give you the desires of your heart? Did I not tell you that all I have is yours? You are mine. You will always be mine. Nothing or no one can take you out of My hand. I love you."

There is a time to listen, a time to speak, and a time to understand. *Selah.* As we tune in to the heart of our beloved, we know when it is time to wait and listen, and we know when it is our turn to speak. The Holy Spirit, our helper, reveals this to us. Knowing when to listen and when to speak is an essential part of effective communication.

Giving Voice to Your Heart

How many times have you said something to someone, realizing and desperately wishing the moment it came out of your mouth that you could somehow retract, rewind or reword it? I've had my share of those times. I've said things, and had things spoken to me that were not "seasoned with love," and it is not a good feeling. Remember whatever we say or do should be graced with His love. It's about the heart. In order to go deeper with God, we have to engage Him with our heart; it cannot be superficial. The world is filled with superficiality. The best place I know to practice "giving voice to your heart" is in the secret place … the place of solitude with Him.

Many times the words of love we rehearse in our minds, as precious as they may be, never make it past our lips to become released into the atmosphere. There is power in the spoken word, and if what you're releasing is expressed with love, it carries exponential power. Don't hold back your words of love to Him. It may sound a little strange to your ears in the beginning, but don't worry. You can train your voice to speak words of love that will soon become second nature to you. Tell Him you love Him, you want more of Him and tell Him what He means to you; tell Him. Don't be afraid to "voice" what is in your heart. You may want to sing aloud to Him, to hum to Him, or just say His name with love.

Don't be afraid to speak what you feel. God knows everything about you anyway, but He wants to hear what's on your heart *from you*. You're His beloved! He likes it when you're real with Him. Tell Him your fears, your frustrations, your worries, and your disappointments. Tell Him your hopes, your desires, your dreams, and whatever else is hidden in your heart. He's a safe God. When you voice what is in your heart it opens you up to trust Him. It frees you in a way that nothing else can, and it produces power because it liberates and breaks confinement.

Conversation with God is a divine exchange. You receive nourishment from the words He speaks, and you give nourishment from the words you speak. And while your words are giving nourishment to God, they are making a powerful declaration to the enemy of your soul. Proverbs 6:2 (NIV) says, "You have been trapped by what you said, ensnared by the words of your mouth." When our words are not in agreement with what God says about us, it can cause much trouble. If we are releasing words from our heart in agreement with God's heart, the lies of the enemy are being destroyed with our affirmation.

ೀ

Prayer and Declaration: Lord, I confess and repent that I have not allowed myself to speak freely from my heart.

Many times, I have held back because of fear and doubt, sometimes even pride. Lord, I confess and repent because I know there are things in my heart that do not line up with what you say about me. I have believed the lies of the enemy. But, no more, Lord. I decree I will speak freely from this point on, and not hold back my words of love to you. I declare I will recognize every lie of the enemy when it comes, and not come in agreement with it, but only come in agreement with what you say, Lord. I declare that not only will I come in agreement with what you say about me, Lord, but I will come in agreement with what you say about everyone I come in contact with, and the words that come out of my mouth will give life and strength and encouragement to the hearer. In Jesus' name, I pray, amen and amen.

⊙⊙

Yielding Your Soul Man

One of the most important things in communicating with God is to understand that we have been made in His image. He, too, has a mind, will, and emotions. He is not some supernatural entity that cannot be touched with feelings. "For we do not have a High Priest who cannot sympathize with our weaknesses, but was in all points tempted as we are, yet without sin." (Hebrews 4:15) One of the most important things to Him is to have fellowship with the ones He has created.

What do you think of when you hear the term "soul mate"? Do you know Jesus wants to be your soul mate? He wants your soul—your mind, will, and emotions—to be one with His. He wants your mind, will, and emotions in agreement with His. This soul mate connection also involves coming to the same conclusion as He does about any given issue because you have the same reasoning process. Communicating with Him as His soul mate builds a strong foundation of trust and love. It is another level of knowing Him and experiencing His power through intimacy.

Ask yourself these questions as you focus on building your relationship with the Lord: What is He feeling? What is He saying? What is He thinking? Engage your senses as you spend time with Him. Many times, you will experience things that are a little unusual, but it is His way of showing you He is near. It could be a tingling in your hands, or maybe a fragrance or aroma you hadn't noticed before. It could be a taste in your mouth like honey or something you see that is beyond your natural vision. Let all of your senses be activated to know and experience Him. I have come to know and love Him in a much greater way by experiencing Him with all of my senses. It has also caused me to understand His holiness, purity, and character to a much greater degree.

Several years ago, while at a Friday evening worship service at my home church, I had gone to the altar to connect with the Lord in a deeper way. His presence was so strong at one point that I could no longer stand. While on the floor, I sensed Jesus came to me and knelt beside me. He was gazing intently at my heart, and then He reached out and retrieved a piece of my heart that had been disconnected from the rest, and put it back in place. Again, He studied my heart, reached out, retrieved another piece that I had "given away" at some point, and put it back in its rightful place. He did that several times, and then He took my whole heart into His hands and began to re-shape and re-mold it. What a beautiful experience that was! When I got up off the floor, I was overwhelmed and elated at the feeling of being made complete again.

That is exactly what He wants to do with all of us. Are there areas of your life that you have prioritized over Him? Maybe something you consider more important, or something you don't want to give up that hinders Him being first in your life? If so, that is an area in which you have given away a portion of your heart. Maybe you've never considered it in such a way, but God is a jealous God. He wants our hearts to be first and foremost His. Give Him all your heart. You won't regret it.

☙

Prayer and Declaration: Father, I confess that I have had other soul mates that I thought would satisfy, but they have not. There have been many things in my life I have chased after, thinking they would satisfy, but they haven't. There has always been something missing. Lord, I repent that I've tried to find my fulfillment in everything but you. Please forgive me, Lord, and take my heart now. Put back the missing pieces that will make me complete again. I declare that as my heart is made whole again, I will use it to glorify and love you. I declare I will be your soul mate Lord. I will be the one you can share everything with. Furthermore, I decree as I press into you with my whole heart, that I will begin to experience you with all of my senses. I decree my whole body, soul, and spirit will become one with you, my beloved Lord. In your name, I pray, amen and amen.

☙❧

Gazing Upon Him

Webster's dictionary defines *gaze* as "to look steadily or intently, as with great curiosity, interest, pleasure or wonder." Have you ever fixed your gaze upon Jesus with the expectation of really seeing Him? Are you looking for Him with eyes of faith? It is only in gazing upon Him that we begin to understand who we have been created to be. If the old saying is true that you become what you look upon, what are your eyes and heart fixed upon?

As we spend time with Him, He will whisper to us who we are, and how He sees us. He will demonstrate His love for us. These truths will become reality as we spend more time with Him. There is nothing that compares with knowing how He sees us, because once we understand His thoughts toward us and about us, it gives us a deep sense of worth and of being loved. How He sees us is truth. Jesus sees with perfect understanding and discernment in all things. In his workbook on *Song of Solomon*, Mike Bickle writes, "A judge may have all the facts about a case but if he has an unclean heart, he will misinterpret the information ..." Jesus has a heart of purity, and everything He sees He judges rightly. As we fix our gaze upon Him, we will be able to see ourselves as He sees us.

"Looking unto Jesus, the author and finisher of our faith, who for the joy that was set before Him endured the cross, despising [disregarding] the shame, and has sat down at the right hand of the throne of God." (Hebrews 12:2) In gazing upon Him, we understand it is us He was thinking about when He went to the cross. He saw into the future, into a day when we would become His. A day we would be overcome with His majesty and beauty and unable to take our eyes off Him. He saw love fulfilled. He saw a bride that would love Him, as He deserves to be loved.

There is another benefit to gazing upon Him. He is our bridegroom King, the one who subdues nations and rules over the whole universe, yet is completely undone by a bride who looks to Him. "You have ravished My heart, My sister, My spouse; you have ravished My heart, with one look of your eyes." (Song of Solomon 4:9) Now consider, if He is so ravished by one glance from us, how is He going to feel when we fix our gaze upon Him? Have you ever put a demand on His attention? It is possible, you know. It is a powerful reality when we begin to gaze upon Him and experience the impact we have on His heart. In that reality, He will say, "What is your petition? It shall be granted you." (Esther 5:6) As it is in the natural realm, so it is in the spirit. It is in the heart of a husband to give his wife what she wants, especially when she comes to him in the context of intimacy.

ॐ

Prayer and Declaration: Lord, forgive me that I have gotten my eyes off you and focused on so many other things. Lord, I repent for allowing my eyes to wander foolishly and spend precious time on searching for things and people to satisfy when only you can satisfy. I repent Lord, that I set time limits on you. If I don't hear from you in my short allotted time, I begin to search elsewhere. I declare from this day forward my eyes will be set apart for you. I declare I will set my gaze upon you, Lord, and search for the answers I need. I decree that you are giving me the wisdom to wait as long as it takes. Additionally, Lord, you are doing so much more than I am even aware of. Thank you, Lord, for the power of my gaze upon your heart. Use my eyes, Lord, for your glory. In Jesus' name, I pray, amen and amen.

ॐ

Seeing Him for Who He Is

Song of Solomon 5:10-16 is a description of our beloved Jesus as seen through the eyes of His bride. Once we understand who He really is and that His heart is for us, all fear of intimacy will dissipate. Below is my understanding of what these verses reveal about Him. As you search Him out for yourself, your understanding of Him will grow and far surpass what has been written here.

Jesus is a born leader; His leadership is perfect. I can always trust Him because He has no hidden agendas. His leadership is of the highest excellence, so I never have to fear being misled or hurt. When I experience His perfect leadership coupled with His love, it breaks any fear of being able to trust Him. Have you ever had your trust broken or been hurt by someone you love? I have but we never have to worry about that with Him. (vv. 10-11)

Jesus' dedication to us is like none other. He is forever dedicated to me; I can count on it. I am in covenant with Him, and He does not break His covenant. Even when I am weak and break covenant … He does not. Because I know He will never leave me or forsake me, I never fear being alone. "…I am with you always, even to the end of the age." (Matthew 28:20) Have you ever been abandoned by someone you love? I have; but that will never happen with Him. (v. 11)

And His eyes! When He looks at me, He sees with perfect discernment. He knows everything about me; the good, the bad, and the ugly, and still loves me deeply. His eyes see the "Yes" in my spirit, even when I fail. His discernment comes from heart purity, and He has righteous, loving motives toward me. Knowing He has perfect discernment breaks the fear of being misunderstood or rejected. Have you ever been misunderstood or rejected? I'm sure we all have, but not with Him. (v. 12)

Have you had days when you feel like you're on an emotional roller coaster? It could be circumstances, hormones, or maybe just a bad hair day! We've all had them. But not so with Jesus. There is perfect balance in his emotions. Since He has a balanced personality, His emotions are always in perfect balance. No emotional roller coaster. Knowing this, our emotions can be brought into wholeness. Have you ever had your emotions shredded by someone's words or actions? You don't have to worry about that with Jesus. He will never toy with your emotions. (v. 13a)

And His words ... talk about a love language! His words are sweet, tender, and pure. If He needs to correct me about anything, He does it with kindness and tenderness. There is no judgment in His correction, only concern for my best. Because of this, His words heal my heart. His words are as a healing balm poured into the wounds of my heart.

Have you ever been hurt by someone's words? Probably, but His words will never hurt. (v. 13b)

Jesus has a beautiful heart of compassion that is so tender. There are times in my life I really struggle, sometimes due to circumstances or negative emotions, but it is so wonderful to know He relates to my struggles with kindness and compassion. He relates because there is nothing I experience that He has not already gone through. "For we do not have a High Priest who cannot sympathize with our weaknesses, but was in all points tempted as we are, yet without sin." (Hebrews 4:15) This realization causes me to love Him even more. Do you want someone who can relate to you on your deepest level? Then look to Him. (v. 14)

"For I know the plans and thoughts I have for you," says the Lord, "Plans for peace and well-being and not for disaster to give you a future and a hope." (Jeremiah 29:11 AMP) God's plans never fail. Not even under pressure. They are designed to give me hope. And because I have hope, it gives me confidence for my future. We all need confidence for the future, especially in these challenging times. How is your confidence level for the future? If it is not where it needs to be, then allow Him to impart His hope and carry out His plans for you. (v. 15)

Lastly, one of the favorite things about my beloved is His very presence. When I'm with Him, I see, feel, and understand by experience who He is. Jesus is full of purity, passion, and love, all mixed together. When I experience Him, it causes me to love Him more. And because I love Him more, I feel safe opening my heart to Him. As I do, we begin to have a dialogue, an intimate communication of our hearts. It is the deepest part of my heart communing with the deepest part of His. It's a sweet experience; there is nothing else so satisfying. Have you ever experienced His tangible presence touching your heart in a deep and profound way? "His mouth is most sweet. Yes, He is altogether lovely. This is my beloved, and this is my friend, O daughters of Jerusalem." (Song of Solomon 5:16) This verse sums up the way we feel about our beloved. The daughters of Jerusalem mentioned here are those who have not yet experienced Him in an intimate way.

What I've touched on in this chapter is the revelation I have received from Song of Solomon 5:10-16 about who He is. It has calmed many of my fears and allowed me to open my heart in ways I previously never could. He is our magnificent God and bridegroom King for all of eternity, and He's crazy about me. He feels the same about you, too. Give Him a chance to show you.

Communication That Goes Beyond Words

It was September 2001, several days after the 9/11 tragedy in our nation. I had gone with several friends to a conference at the International House of Prayer in Kansas City, hosted by Mike Bickle. There was a lot of unrest and uneasiness in our nation and people during this time, but I felt so strongly the Lord calling me to "come away" with Him. So, in spite of the all the turmoil, I went.

During one of the evening sessions, there was an altar call and I went forward. Someone prayed for me and as Holy Spirit overwhelmed me, I found myself on the floor. Instantly, the Lord gave me a vision and followed it up with a tangible experience that left me completely undone. Not only has it made a lasting impact on my life, but has set me on a course to pursue Him for the rest of my life.

In the vision, I was at the banqueting table with Jesus, and there were a lot of people at the table, but He was sitting directly across from me. He looked at me and said, "What do you want?" I was delighted because I knew I could have anything I asked for. I said, "Oh, Lord; that my husband would come to know you in a deeper way!" A moment passed, and once again He spoke, "What else do you want?" Again, I knew I could have whatever I wanted, and so I said, "Oh, Lord; that my children would come to know you in a deeper way!" He paused a moment and then, looking at me intently, said, "What else do you want?" At that moment, rather taken aback that He asked a third time, I looked deep into His eyes. They were like a fiery, burning liquid love. It was as if I were looking into them for the very first time, and they were the most beautiful, piercing eyes I had ever seen. They touched the very depths of my soul.

I said to Him, "Oh Lord, I just want more of you!" When I said that, He suddenly was right there in front of me. We were no longer at the table but standing face-to-face. He laid me back in His arms and I was looking up into His fiery eyes, and then He "overshadowed me" with His presence. I felt His glory radiating within my whole being as if He were imparting His very glory within me. I saw, felt, and actually experienced just how beautiful He was. This experience of His manifested glory being poured over and into me lasted for what seemed like an eternity, and I had no concept of time or surroundings, only His glory radiating within my entire body, soul, and spirit. This experience was a divine impartation of His character, holiness, and purity.

Eventually my friends lifted me up and carried me back to my hotel room. All I could do was weep and say, "He is so beautiful, He is so beautiful!" I did not sleep that night, but just lay across my bed, feeling His glory and very being still radiating within me.

This experience of His glory emanating within me lasted until late the next afternoon, and caused me to love Him in a way I never knew was possible. Even though I had accepted the Lord as my Savior twenty years earlier, this experience caused me to know Him and His greatness in a much deeper way. The experience of His glory created an unquenchable fire in my soul to pursue Him, and set me on a quest to seek Him for the rest of my life because I know there is more. There is always more of Him.

This type of experience is an example of communication that goes beyond words. These types of experiences can release a greater measure of His love, increase our faith, give us a new depth of understanding, and cause our hearts to yearn for more. To quote Pastor Jerry Howell at Destiny Christian Center, "A person with a spiritual experience is never at the mercy of a person with a theological argument." There is much truth in that statement.

There are numerous examples in scripture of communication that goes beyond words. Joseph had dreams, Daniel saw visions, Peter experienced trances, and Paul was overcome by the presence of the Lord on the road to Damascus. Mary was overshadowed by Holy Spirit and gave birth to Jesus. Mary of Bethany poured out her precious alabaster box of perfume over Jesus and then carried that fragrance with her wherever she went. These are all forms of communication that go beyond words. The Lord has put His seal of approval on every type of communication that brings Him glory. I believe there are forms that we have yet to experience. I say 'YES!' to everything that will honor and glorify Him. What about you?

❧

Prayer and Declaration: Lord, I understand there is communication with you that goes beyond words, and I understand this communication can take on many different forms. Although I do not seek experiences, Lord, I want to experience more of you. Forgive me for times I have not made room for more of you, Lord. Forgive me for being in a hurry to be about my own business and missing opportunities with you. I declare, Lord, that I will be open to any experience you want to give me, because I know, Lord, that as it comes from you, it will reveal your character and nature, and cause me to love you more. In Jesus' name, I pray, amen and amen.

❧

Reflections on Chapter Two

1. How can you show more of God's love in your communication?

_____

_____

_____

_____

_____

_____

_____

_____

2. Name three ways to yield more fully to the Lord with your body, soul, and spirit.

_____

_____

_____

_____

_____

_____

_____

_____

3. List at least three ways you want to communicate with God in a new way.

_____

_____

_____

_____

_____

_____

_____

_____

_____

CHAPTER 3

God's Original Desires

Have you ever asked yourself the question, "What is in God's heart? What does He want?" You might say, "Well, He is God. He doesn't need anything. He's got everything He wants and needs." He owns the whole universe, but there is one thing He doesn't have. He has made man with a free will to choose, and we have a choice to receive Him or not receive Him. His desire is that we would choose Him. God wants to fellowship and have a relationship with us. When God created the heavens and earth and put man in the garden, it was so He could walk with man in the cool of the day. God loved the fellowship He had with Adam and Eve. He loved His relationship with Abraham and His closeness with Moses. David's worship caused God to pen him as a man after His own heart, and Esther was a woman that captured God's heart. The Shulamite caused Him to be lovesick, and when God came to earth in the form of the man Jesus, His desire was still to draw close to those He loved. He spent many hours with His disciples and loved them unconditionally. He had a special place in His heart for Mary, as well as Lazarus and others close to Him. When Jesus was taken back up to heaven, He sent the Holy Spirit because He still wanted to be close to His people. "For God so loved the world that He gave His only begotten Son, that whoever believes in Him should not perish, but have everlasting life." (John 3:16)

Jesus is not coming back for a cold, stoic church, but He's coming for a passionate bride who has Him on her mind. Once more, it is not about gender, but it's about *position*. A bride co-reigns with her bridegroom. She knows His agenda, His thoughts, His dreams, and His pain. She is an extension of Him and His agenda. She takes no thought for her agenda because her passion is wrapped up in His.

One morning while reading God's word, He gave me a whole new revelation of the rhema word He had given me when I first got saved, which was actually my very first rhema word. A *rhema* word is simply a verse or portion of Scripture that the Holy Spirit enlightens to your mind and understanding, and in the Greek means "utterance, or the living voice of God". "You did not choose Me, but I chose you and appointed you that you should go and bear fruit, and that your fruit should remain, that whatever you ask the Father in My name, He may give you." (John 15:16)

I originally thought the fruit He spoke about in John 15:16 was bearing fruit for others to enjoy. But this particular day, I understood the fruit we bear is for Him. He desires to "eat" the fruit of our life that we may be one. The scripture He gave to confirm what I was hearing is Song of Solomon 4:16: "Let My beloved come into His garden and eat its choicest fruits." Here the Shulamite, otherwise known as the bride of Christ, is asking her beloved bridegroom to come into the garden of her life and partake of her best fruit. It is fruit that can only be produced as she abides in Him and He abides in her. This fruit is sweet to His taste and satisfies Him greatly. That's why it is "choice" fruit. It gratifies His desire that we may be one and partner together with Him. *Selah*.

"A garden enclosed is my sister, my spouse. A spring shut up, a fountain sealed. A fountain of gardens, a well of living waters, and streams from Lebanon." (Song of Solomon 4:12, 15) When Jesus looks at us, He sees us as a garden full of lush fruit, beautiful fountains and all kinds of wonderful vegetation. This garden is a place He delights to come, and it gives Him great pleasure. It is a place for the two of us to sup, fellowship, and enjoy one another. In our lives, everything we do and everything we are should first be for Him. Even bearing fruit should line up with the first commandment. He desires to partake of the fruit of our lives. Are you allowing the Lord to partake of the fruit in your garden? Or is your garden unkempt and grown over with weeds? Have you cultivated the garden of your soul and spirit, or neglected it?

ॐ

Prayer and Declaration: Father, forgive me for the times I have forgotten that you just want to be with me. Forgive me for not giving you first place in my life and taking the time for fellowship with you and you alone. I repent for the times I really haven't thought too much about you or your desires. Lord, help my unbelief and lack of consideration for you. I declare from this day forward I will produce choice fruit in my life to serve you. Lord, I declare my life will be an offering to you for your purposes. I want my passion to be wrapped up in yours. In Jesus' name, I pray, amen and amen.

ॐ

Foundational Obedience

When you hear the word obedience, what do you think of? Most people think of a list of do's and don'ts. We can't do this, we shouldn't do that. We have to do this; we're not allowed to do that. Sound familiar? God is revealing to us an obedience that has nothing to do with rules. It is an attitude of the heart. He says in scripture, "…I will put my laws in their minds and will write it on their hearts…." (Jeremiah 31:33) To have His law in your mind takes the guesswork out of right and wrong. But to have His law written on your heart has a much deeper meaning. If His law is written on your heart, there is an element of undeniable covenant. There has to be a mutual agreement for something to be written on your heart. There is no struggle when your heart is in agreement with His law of life. This type of obedience is a beautiful thing.

Foundational obedience takes this truth a little deeper. Foundational obedience is the cornerstone of obedience, and it stems from the first commandment: "… you shall love the Lord your God with all your heart, with all your soul, with all your strength, and with all your mind…." (Luke 10:27) Listen, the only way we can love Him the way this scripture admonishes us to, is to really know Him. Foundational obedience is being quick to come away with Him when we hear Him call, just because He is more important to us than anything else. Many of us have a set time to spend with God, but there are moments outside of that designated time that God wants to be with us. It may not be a convenient time in the natural realm, but nevertheless, He wants to draw us aside with Him. He wants to share the secrets of His heart and sometimes just be with us. First of all, we must have ears to hear the Holy Spirit when those gentle urgings come. But that's only the beginning. Secondly, we have to be willing to drop whatever we are doing to come aside. It may be just for a moment, time enough for us to feel His sweet kiss on our heart, or it may be He has a secret He wants to reveal. It may be He wants to exhort or warn us about something. We don't really know, but we will miss the opportunity if we say, "I'm too busy right now. I'll come in a little while." Foundational obedience is so important! How many missed opportunities have we had? We say we love Him, we say He's number one ... but is He?

Foundational obedience is the true test of our love and commitment. In the book of Esther, Queen Vashti was too busy when the king called her; she was having her own party. My friends, that party cost her dearly. She was stripped of her royal position and banished from the King's presence forever. Let's learn from her mistake. I am in no way implying God would punish us in that way, but the fact is, if we miss an opportunity in His presence, we have missed something very valuable. He knows we are human beings, full of frailties. But listen, to come immediately when He calls delights His heart, and He will do anything for the one He delights in. Let's be quick to answer when He calls, and then give Him our undivided attention. He has something to say.

How many know it is possible to be in a place physically, but to not be there in heart or soul? Many times have I been guilty of being in the secret place, only to find my mind wandering, considering the day ahead and things I need to accomplish. When God calls at inopportune times, it is not easy to give Him our full attention; but in not doing so, we miss out on some of the greatest truths and experiences He has to offer us. Part of foundational obedience is being one hundred percent engaged when you come aside with Him. Give Him all of who you are, so He can pour into you all of what He has at that moment. The rewards of being in the moment with Him are unlimited.

☙

Prayer and Declaration: Lord there are so many things vying for my time and attention, but I know none of these things will satisfy like you do. Forgive me for putting so many things ahead of you in importance. Forgive me for not coming when I feel the prompting of the Holy Spirit, thinking I just have to get this done or do this one thing first. I repent, Lord, for not putting you first. Deep down I know, Lord, that you are the answer to everything. I want you first in my life. I want to come immediately when you call. I know as I do I will find my life is richer and fuller than if I had delayed. I also know, Lord, that you will be my time manager. You understand my responsibilities and commitments, and you will direct and prosper my every step as I put you first. Lord, I declare you are giving me a heart of foundational obedience, and I will begin to recognize the gentle urgings of the Holy Spirit to come away with you. And I declare Lord, that my heart will say "Yes" to you, even at inopportune times. I know there will be a great reward in my obedience. And I decree,

Lord, that I will come to a place of delighting when you call because I know you have something special to give. In Jesus' name, I pray, amen and amen.

☙

Redeemed Choices

There are times we can find ourselves in difficult places due to choices we make that are not always good. They are sometimes made out of selfish desires and lead us down the wrong path; but if your heart is to follow the Lord, He will take those choices and turn them for good. He will allow us to see and experience how our choice has affected us, and as we are quick to repent, He will set things in order.

The following is a vision the Lord gave me during of those times, and is such a good example of how He can turn things around quickly and redeem our choices. It was a Friday afternoon and because of wrong choices I had made that led to guilt and condemnation, I had decided not to go to church that Friday night. Now I have always loved going to church to worship on Friday night, but not this particular night. I was in a bad place mentally and emotionally. About 4:30 p.m., I went to my prayer room and began to press into the Lord. After a short time, He gave me the gift of repentance. It went so deep in my spirit it is hard to explain, but I knew this spirit of repentance was a gift from Him. It wasn't something I could have produced on my own, but it was my spirit of brokenness and humility, connecting with His Spirit of reconciliation. I have never experienced the *gift* of repentance to that degree before. I was on the floor for about forty-five minutes to an hour, just weeping and travailing, and then He gave me the vision.

I was lying on the ground as though I had been knocked down. I was dressed in a wedding gown and had a crown that had fallen off. Jesus came and picked me up, brushed me off and picked up my crown, put it back on my head, and straightened it. Then He put His arms around me and held me for a few minutes. There was such healing in that embrace. He then smiled and took my hand and we started up the mountain together. When we did, I heard a scripture reference in my spirit, and then the vision ended. I pondered that vision a few minutes and then read the scripture, which impacted me greatly:

> For who is God except the Lord? Or who is the rock save our God? The God who girds me with strength and makes my way perfect? He makes my feet like hinds' feet [able to stand firmly or make progress on the dangerous heights of testing and trouble]; He sets me securely upon my high places. He teaches my hands to war, so that my arms can bend a bow of bronze. You have also given me the shield of your salvation, and your right hand has held me up; your gentleness and condescension have made me

great. You have given plenty of room for my steps under me, that my feet would not slip. I pursued my enemies and overtook them; neither did I turn again until they were consumed. I smote them so that they were not able to rise; they fell wounded under my feet. For you have girded me with strength for the battle; you have subdued under me and caused to bow down those who rose up against me. You have also made my enemies turn their backs to me, that I might cut off those who hate me. They cried [for help], but there was none to deliver—even unto the Lord, but He answered them not. Then I beat them small as the dust before the wind; I emptied them out as the dirt and mire of the streets.

Psalm 18: 31-42, AMP

When I read verse 37 (I pursued my enemies and overtook them; neither did I turn again until they were consumed), He told me that was my assignment for the evening. I knew I was to go to church because my assignment was to enter into the dance of worship and spiritual warfare against my enemies. Those enemies, just to name a few, were fear, guilt, shame, and discouragement. And even though Jesus didn't say this, I felt that as I was obedient to the assignment, I would see a release of His power as the enemy fell. So I got ready, put my warfare dance clothes on, and set my eyes "like flint" on my assignment. I have worshiped in the dance many times in my church, but this time was different. On the way to church, I asked God for the anointing to worship Him, which I had never prayed before. By the time I got to church, I felt so empowered for my mission that I don't think anyone or anything could have stopped me.

And God was so faithful! Towards the end of the service, our worship leader began to sing about the Christian soldiers, and our heart and our sword. As I prophetically "swung my sword," I knew the victory had been secured and my enemies had fallen. Shortly after that, miraculous healings began to take place, and people in the congregation came to the altar to be healed and to receive a new anointing. A heavenly portal was opened as our enemies fell.

When I left the service, I was "drunk" in the spirit and stayed that way until about 4:00 a.m. in the morning. What an incredible ending to what started out as a very hard day! It caused me to stand in awe of God's faithfulness and goodness. He makes a way even when there doesn't seem to be a way.

The vision and word He gave me earlier in the day was proof to me that even when we make wrong choices, God can redeem those choices. And on looking back, I believe the assignment He gave me was to reinforce the spiritual reality that we have victory over our enemies. As I was faithful to that assignment, He caused my enemies to fall and become as nothing, and then He set my feet back on the right path.

☙❧

Prayer and Declaration: Father, I thank you that even when we don't choose correctly, you extend your love and grace to us. Thank you that you are compassionate and gracious, slow to anger, and abounding in love. I pray, Lord, to be ever mindful of my choices, and to always attempt to choose wisely. I pray that my heart will always be in tune with yours, and that I will never grieve or quench the Holy Spirit knowingly. I declare, Lord, that even when we miss the mark, you have a way of redemption. I declare that as your people recognize the power of repentance, they will also recognize the spiritual reality that we have victory over our enemies through repentance. Our warfare may look different ways at different times, but you will always lead us on the right path, Lord. I declare we will know when it is our battle, and when we should stand still because it is your battle, Lord. And Father, I declare the power of a clean heart will always lead us in the way of righteousness and victory. In Jesus' mighty name, amen and amen.

☙❧

Seeing with Eyes of Vision

I was once again in the sanctuary, and our pastor was reading from the book of Revelation about the throne room. He gave an altar call to come and stand on the sea of glass. I went to the altar and felt compelled to lay face down, imagining I was on the sea of glass. I suddenly found myself in a vision "transported" underneath the sea of glass, actually submerged in it. I saw all the brilliant colors in the throne room, reflecting into the transparent water. The colors were swirling all around me, beautiful, vivid and alive. They were flowing into one another. I looked up and the colors were above and beneath the sea of glass, like there was no separation at all. Then the vision ended and I heard the Lord say, "Now may the eyes of your understanding be enlightened." *Selah*.

One of the great apostolic prayers of the Apostle Paul says:

> … that the God of our Lord Jesus Christ, the Father of glory, may give to you the spirit of wisdom and revelation in the knowledge of Him, the eyes of your understanding being enlightened; that you may know what is the hope of His calling, what are the riches of the glory of His inheritance in the saints, and what is the exceeding greatness of His power toward us who believe, according to the working of His mighty power which He worked in Christ when He raised Him from the dead and seated Him at His right hand in the heavenly places, far above all principality and power and might and dominion, and every name that is named, not only in this age but also in that which is to come. And He put all things under His

feet and gave Him to be head over all things to the church, which is His body, the fullness of Him who fills all in all.

Ephesians 1:17-22

This prayer is so full of revelation, I just wonder if the apostle knew or even considered the impact it would have on the body and bride of Christ in the ages to come. In verse eighteen of this great prayer, Paul speaks specifically about our understanding. He prays the eyes of our understanding would be enlightened. Enlightened to what? Enlightened to know the hope He has called us to. Enlightened to the fact that we are His inheritance. Have you considered you are the inheritance of the creator of the universe? That should make you feel pretty special! Paul also prays that we would understand the *dunamis* power that He has given us. The same power He gave to Christ. Wow! If we can grasp the reality that all these things are His desires for us, how powerful that will be. I don't think we will have any problem running to Him when He calls if we understand this. So, if you want to experience your eyes being enlightened to all this, there is just one requirement. Turn your gaze upon Him. Fix your eyes and your heart of understanding upon Him.

๙๑๏

Prayer and Declaration: Lord, I want to gaze upon you. I want my eyes to be fixed on you. I understand there is so much you want to give me, so much you want to do. Forgive me for the distractions that I have allowed, the things I have put before you. Lord, I repent for the times you have allowed me to see something and my spiritual eyes have been so dull. Lord, I choose to give you my eyes. I declare, Lord, that the eyes of my understanding will be enlightened by Holy Spirit to comprehend not only what you're showing me, but the significance of it. And Lord, I decree my eyes will be flooded with your light, and everything I see will line up with the way you see things. In Jesus' name, amen and amen.

༺༻

A Hearing Ear

In Mark 4:9 Jesus says, "He who has ears to hear, let Him hear." And again in Revelation 3:22, "He who has an ear, let him hear what the Spirit says…" There are several places in scripture Jesus talked about ears to hear, and it is because God wants our ears in tune to Him. He has many things to tell us and mysteries He wants to reveal. If we are not listening, we will miss it. There are many times the Lord will speak to me in a gentle whisper, and I must have my ears waiting and tuned in, or I will miss it. Do you know it is possible to live in a place where our spirit is in constant communion with His Spirit? This type of communion will come as we "practice" listening on a regular basis. After a lot of practice, it becomes second nature and something we are not even aware of on a natural level, but yet our spirit is always actively listening. It is one of those mysteries that cannot be explained, but experiencing it will remove any doubt of what you should say or do in a given situation.

In the natural realm, is there someone you love who makes your heart beat a little faster when you hear them? That's the way it is with a bride who is in love with her bridegroom. She longs to hear his voice, and when there is any amount of time they are away from each other, the sound of his voice is like honey to her ears.

Do you feel that way towards your heavenly bridegroom? Are your ears straining to hear His whisper? Are you in a posture of listening? To be in a posture of listening is an act of faith. It pleases Him when you have an expectation to hear Him. To those who say He doesn't talk to them or they don't hear Him, there are probably many distractions that are "catching" your ear, and too much activity drowning out His voice. Proverbs 2:2 says "…incline your ear to wisdom." The result of inclining your ear is in Proverbs 2:5: "Then you will understand the fear of the Lord, and find the knowledge of God." Who are you inclining your ear to? What is it that you have a tendency to listen to? *Selah.*

His words carry such power. One word from Him can melt the coldest heart, heal the deepest hurt, and fill the most painful void. And all we have to do is listen. Listen with our ears and with our heart. There is a difference between listening with your reasoning, your carnal mind, and listening with your heart. Listening with your heart will take some practice. But it will be worth every minute you spend. Practice the art of listening for your beloved. Practice His presence in the recesses of your heart. Be aware of His presence abiding in you and listen … He has something to say and secrets to share, and you are the one He wants to share them with.

ॐ

Prayer and Declaration: Lord, I thank you that there is a promise for those who will hear you. I pray to always have my ear tuned to you for instruction and guidance. I pray, Lord, that you will make me aware of the times that other voices are drowning out your voice. Father, I declare you have given me ears to hear, and I will hear you throughout my day. I declare other voices will not take precedence over your voice, and other sounds will not drown out your voice, Lord. And I decree as I hear your voice, I will also understand with perfect discernment what you are saying and what I should do. In Jesus' mighty name, amen and amen.

ॐ

The Language of Love

"Let Him kiss me with the kisses of His mouth…" (Song of Solomon 1:2) This verse in scripture portrays the heart of a ravished bride calling for a kiss, or the touch of her beloved bridegroom's spirit upon her heart. Have you ever felt the kiss of His word upon your heart? It is apparent in this verse that the bride has experienced His kiss in a deep way and desires more. There is nothing God would love more than to know we desire the kisses of His mouth. The phrase "the kisses of His mouth" is a metaphor, meaning in the spiritual sense it is His touch, or the Holy Spirit's touch upon our heart. It is the release of His word that tenderizes and draws our heart. For example, have you ever been reading God's word and had a portion just leap out at you? Maybe it is something you have been praying to receive, to know, or to understand. And suddenly, it comes alive. That is a *rhema* word. That is the word of God that speaks to your heart individually; it becomes living and active in your heart. The kiss of His word is the written word, or it can be His spoken word to you that becomes personal and intimate. When you experience this, God is "kissing" you with the "kisses of His word, or His mouth." There are other ways to receive His kiss in addition to the written word. God can speak to you in numerous ways through a thought, a picture, a prayer, or someone else's words. If you are in tune with Him, you will know when His kiss comes.

Let's take it a step further. When you want His kiss and ask for it, God's heart will be completely undone. What would delight His heart more than His bride wanting His kiss, and even asking for it? Asking for His kiss is a demonstration of your love and will touch His heart very deeply. But that's just the way love is … finding mutual satisfaction and joy in pleasing the one your heart longs to be with.

God wants to hear our voice. He wants us to express our love for Him. "O my dove, in the clefts of the rock, in the secret places of the cliff, let me see your face, let me hear your voice; for your voice is sweet, and your face is lovely." (Song of Solomon 2:14) While we can speak to God in many different ways, there is a heavenly bridal language that is meant for you and God alone. Have you discovered it yet? The heavenly bridal language is the gift God gives us when we receive His Holy Spirit. Paul says in I Corinthians 14:2, "For he who speaks in a tongue does not speak to men but to God, for no one understands him; however, in the Spirit he speaks mysteries."

In your times alone with God, speaking in tongues for His ears only is truly a bridal language that will take us to new heights in the spirit. Romans 8: 26-27 says: "… for we do not know what we should pray for as we ought, but the Spirit Himself makes intercession for us with groanings which cannot be uttered. Now He who searches the hearts knows what the mind of the Spirit is, because He makes intercession for the saints according to the will of God."

You don't know how precious your bridal language is to God until He floods you with His love while you are speaking to Him in this heavenly language. He responds to what you speak. That flood of love is also His kiss upon your heart. Have you noticed how two people in love have their "own" language? They communicate with one another in a way that is for them alone.

There is a powerful secret regarding the heavenly bridal language that we as His bride are just beginning to touch. God's ways are so much higher than ours, and His thoughts so much higher. The heavenly bridal language is a vehicle, a tool, and many times a weapon of warfare God will use; and is now using to a much greater degree in the end times in which we are now living. It is a higher form of communication that is beyond our current reasoning and frame of reference at this time. I have seen glimpses of the greater power and effectiveness of this language at times. This type of communication with God and with fellow believers is one that the enemy cannot and will not be able to interrupt in any way, shape or form. The bridal language is on a wave-length unlike anything else. It is the sound frequency of the Holy Spirit, and one that God will teach us more about in the days to come. He has many things to teach us as yet. We are living in a time of history where all things are culminating, and there is revelation He is releasing even now that will cause us to be a victorious army moving in love and power. The enemy cannot stop the movement that is coming.

❦

Prayer and Declaration: Lord, my prayer is like the Shulamite's in Song of Solomon: "Kiss me with the kisses of your mouth." I want to know you more Lord. Just as you know me, I want to know you. I want my words to have an intense effect on you. I want them to cause your heart to be captured and undone. I want them to delight you. Just as you are giving me my heart's desire, Lord, I want to give you your heart's desire. Teach me about the heavenly bridal language. Our language, Lord: the one that not only communicates with words, but with heart and soul. It is the language of deep calling unto deep. Lord, I declare the sound of your corporate bride moving in love will cause a shift in the atmosphere, and many will be set free and delivered because of your wisdom. Lord, I declare I am part of that bride; and I will be one who speaks your language and moves with your heart. In your precious name, Jesus, I pray, amen and amen.

❦

A Sealed Heart

God's word says, "Keep your heart with all diligence, for out of it spring the issues of life." (Proverbs 4:23) God cares for our hearts and doesn't want anything coming in that would keep us from His best. He ultimately is our best. As we keep a guard on our heart, and not allow anything to take precedence over our Lord, we can be assured that He will fill our heart with Himself. He will satisfy our heart with His spirit, His emotions, and His attributes. A guarded heart is what Song of Solomon calls a sealed heart. It is our beloved speaking to us His bride, "Set me as a seal upon your heart, as a seal upon your arm …" (Song of Solomon 8:6) The Lord desires to be the seal upon our heart. He also wants to be the seal on our arm, which speaks of our ministry or our work. His seal is a guarantee of His ownership, protection, and authority; but the bride must make the choice to allow Him uninhibited entrance and reign.

He wants our heart to be totally His, first and foremost. Are there things in your life that you've put before Him? If so, then that thing or person has become an idol in your life. We cannot allow anything to take first place in our hearts except Him. If you have, then take a moment and confess those things. Lay those things or people before Him, and ask Him to put them in the proper place in your heart. Confess your need. He first and foremost wants our heart, and the rest will follow.

In his workbook on the *Song of Solomon*, Mike Bickle with the International House of Prayer in Kansas City, Missouri shares several key elements about the Lord's seal on His bride. Unlike the seal of wax used in ancient times, the seal of the Lord is His divine fire released by Holy Spirit. It is God Himself sealing us with His divine love. This love empowers our sinful human hearts and causes us not only to overcome the trials and temptations, but to be able to love Jesus the way Father God loves Him. In John 17:26 Jesus prays to His Father, "the love with which you loved me be in them, and I in them." This is a prayer that Father God will answer. Mike goes on to say that this divine seal is the fire of God and is the most vehement flame. This fiery flame will burn away anything that tries to keep us from His all-consuming divine love. Fire penetrates and purifies. His holy fire will burn away all the dross in our hearts and cause us to burn with fiery love, first towards Him, and then towards His people. God will have a people who burn with love for what He loves. God Himself is a consuming fire.

I had a vision in 2009 in which the Lord showed me His heart, and it was like a huge fiery planet, burning very hot and bright. There were other hearts encircling His, and as far as I could see there were hearts circling His. The whole scene looked like a solar system, but instead of planets, it was hearts. God's fiery heart had a gravitational pull to it, a drawing to Him. Then I saw the hearts closest to His, as they inched nearer because of the gravitational pull, suddenly being sucked into His heart and consumed by the fire. The hearts on the outer perimeter were cold and dark, but as they drew closer to His heart, they would begin to glow from the heat, grow hotter, then ignite and burn, as they were drawn closer and closer to His fiery heart. Once they ignited, they were drawn up into His heart. The hearts just kept coming and coming as far as I could see. They were cold and dark, but one by one, they ignited and were drawn up into His fiery heart, and consumed by Him. The verse I heard the Lord speak concerning this vision was Hebrews 12:29, "… Our God is a consuming fire." Let Him consume you for His plans and purposes.

As our hearts are sealed for Him, we can believe Him not only from our minds, but from our hearts. To believe from your heart is much deeper that believing from your mind because your heart is connected with your spirit man. God knows if He has our heart, the rest will follow. When Jesus was asked what the greatest commandment in the law was, He replied, "You shall love the Lord your God with all your heart, with all your soul, and with all your mind." (Matthew 22:37) It begins with our heart.

As we search for Him with all our heart, there are certain expressions that can best be released when we are in the secret place with Him. Our heart yearnings can be expressed most clearly in the chambers of our King. There is no place as safe and secure as a place alone with Him. It is here we can be completely real and open. No fear of rejection or shame. No fear of misunderstanding or confusion. We know He will understand our heart cry because of His heart of love and purity. Have you heard the invitation into His chambers? Notice *chambers* are not singular, but plural; there are many levels of His chambers. Just when you think you have reached the ultimate, there is still more. Because with God, there is always more.

Prayer, Declaration, and Prophetic Word: Thank you, Lord, for the gift of a romanced, sealed heart that I can carry with me at all times, Thank you, Lord, that because of this, I can walk free from fear and shame. Lord, I ask your forgiveness for not guarding my heart the way I should. I know my heart is precious to you and I repent for the times I have been careless with it. I repent for the times I have given away what is rightfully yours. Lord, I decree right this moment that my heart is yours completely. I declare, Lord, that you will take this imperfect heart and use it for your glory. You said Lord, that we don't have to be perfect, just willing. I decree I am willing. Let our hearts become one. I decree, Lord, that you will consume everything in my heart that is not of you so that I can boldly come into your chambers and discover more and more of your wondrous person. In Jesus' mighty name, amen and amen.

And I hear the Lord saying "I will defeat every enemy that tries to steal your heart from Me. Of that, you can be sure."

An Essential Ingredient: Trust

One of the most basic ingredients in a loving relationship is trust. God wants us to trust Him. The only way we can trust Him is to understand who He really is. To intimately know His attributes, His character, and His love. He is worthy of all our trust, dedication, and love. One of my favorite scriptures which has become *rhema* to me, and one that has steadied me in rocky times has been Proverbs 3:5-6: "Trust in the Lord with all your heart, and lean not on your own understanding; in all your ways acknowledge Him, and He shall direct your paths." The Message version of that scripture says it a little differently: "Trust God from the bottom of your heart; don't try to figure out everything on your own. Listen for God's voice in everything you do, everywhere you go; He's the one who will keep you on track." The trust factor with God is, again, connected to our heart. First our hearts, then our minds. If we will put Him first in every area, He will direct us. His path is the right one and leads us to the highest and best for our lives.

God made man to nurture, care and protect. In the natural realm, a husband wants his wife to trust him. He wants to prove to her that he can provide and care for her, and love her the way she wants and needs to be loved. He also needs to know she respects his wisdom enough to trust him, even when she doesn't agree with his decisions. This involves being able to let go and let him lead, even when she's not sure he is making the right choice. In all relationships, especially marriage, trust is a big factor! If you don't have trust, you're walking on shaky ground.

In the spiritual realm, how do you think God feels when we say "No" to Him because we don't trust Him? Is that equivalent to unbelief? We think "God, I can't trust you on this particular issue because I don't believe you have already made provision for it. This is one of those things, God, you forgot about; you didn't know was going to happen. No, God, I cannot trust you. I have to do this on my own: I have to do it my way." Is that how we think? How that must grieve God's heart, to know we don't trust Him enough to let Him lead. He is our Father, our beloved bridegroom. His leadership over us is perfect. He's completely trustworthy.

Song of Solomon 5:1 describes the leadership of the Lord: "His head is like the finest gold…" What is the finest gold? It is gold that has been purified and refined to a state of excellence. Jesus is the head of the church and His leadership is most excellent. He is a born leader, and He inherited it from His Father. There is no leadership that compares to His. He can be trusted because of His character and the fact that He has no hidden agenda. Have you ever had trouble trusting someone in leadership because you knew their agenda was not what it seemed? Maybe so, but not with Him. Trusting Him breaks any fear of unbelief and doubt, in any situation.

"You will keep him in perfect peace, whose mind is stayed on you, because he trusts in you." (Isaiah 26:3) Here is the secret to perfect peace! Keeping our minds fixed on Him because we trust Him. Do you need peace in your life? Fix your mind on Him. Trust Him. The Voice Bible translation says, "You will keep the peace, a perfect peace, for all who trust in you, for those who dedicate their hearts and minds to you." To dedicate has much the same meaning as the word "holy". To *dedicate* is "to set apart and consecrate to a sacred purpose; to devote wholly and earnestly." As we dedicate our hearts and minds to the One who is perfect peace, we too, will experience the peace that passes all understanding. And it starts with trust.

❧

Prayer and Declaration: Lord, help me to trust you more. Forgive me for the times I have not trusted you because of my own fears. Father, I repent for the unbelief and doubt that has sometimes negated my faith and trust in you. I want to be able to trust you with everything that concerns me. I yield my heart to you, Lord. Philippians 2:13 says that you cause us both to will and to do your good pleasure. I submit to your will and good pleasure in my life, Lord. Show me how to trust you implicitly, Lord, by showing me your true nature and character in my time alone with you. And I declare Lord, as I see and experience who you really are in the secret place of your chambers, I will be able to easily trust you. In Jesus' name, I pray, amen and amen.

❧

A Yielded Vessel

Romans 12:1 says, "I beseech you therefore, brethren, by the mercies of God, that you present your bodies a living sacrifice, holy, acceptable to God, which is your reasonable service." God's desire is that we might become one with Him. When we become one, we are living life to the fullest. We are living the "life more abundantly" that Jesus talked about.

What does it mean to present our bodies as a living sacrifice? Everything we do throughout the day should be a form of worship to Him. It should bring Him honor. Even the mundane things we feel are a waste of time can be done in an attitude of worship. That is presenting our bodies as a living sacrifice, a temple of the Holy Spirit. We must get to the place where the Holy Spirit is *reality* living in us. Did you catch that? The Holy Spirit is reality living in us. Have you ever said or done something that grieved or quenched the Holy Spirit? Of course; we all have. To recognize when the Holy Spirit is quenched or grieved is to ultimately be aware of the one living in us. And it is the Holy Spirit in us that witnesses to the reality of the Father and Son.

As we present our bodies as a living sacrifice to God, He can use us in ways we never imagined. Think about the possibilities if all of our senses were dedicated to Him. Do you want to see into the spirit realm? Do you want to bring into the visible what you see in the invisible? Do you want to hear things others can't, and have the wisdom to know what to do in any given circumstance? This is all possible. But it doesn't come without a price. The price is truly presenting our bodies to Him to be used in whatever way He desires.

As our bodies are presented as a living sacrifice, we can literally smell or sense the aroma of death, or the fragrance of life. There's an aroma or a fragrance that reveals the heart of those we come in contact with. Do you want to partner with God with your sense of smell? It is possible. 2 Corinthians 2:14-15 says, "Now thanks be to God who always leads us in triumph in Christ, and through us diffuses the fragrance of His knowledge in every place. For we are to God the fragrance of Christ among those who are being saved [life] and among those who are perishing [death]." As we allow the Holy Spirit to reign in our bodies, we become the very fragrance of Christ. And because we are in Him, the fragrance of His knowledge can be released wherever we go. Let's choose to carry the fragrance of God within us as we yield to the Holy Spirit. That fragrance produces life.

There have been a number of times I've been in a room, and I sensed the Lord releasing His fragrance. Invariably, people in the room will begin to make comments about the fragrance. I've discovered the scent is not always the same, but it's always a wonderful scent. At times I am able to share what the fragrance is and where it is coming from, and other times I'm not. But every time I am in awe of the Lord and His uniqueness, and the way He is teaching me to be aware of Him. As we become more aware of the Lord through practicing His presence, we will discover the delightful reality that He is always with us, and never leaves us.

Experiencing His fragrance is one of many facets of discovering Him as we become a yielded vessel. One of the meanings of a *vessel* according to Webster's dictionary is "a hollow container or receptacle, used to hold liquids or other contents." As a yielded vessel, we are allowing God to come and fill us with whatever He desires. We can be filled with different things at different times. He may at times fill us with joy and laughter, other times weeping in intercession, and other times a deep reverence and awe to experience His holiness. As the Holy Spirit is allowed free reign, our yielded vessels become a conduit of God's purpose and plan. Being yielded becomes an adventure in the spirit, where life is always fresh and new.

༺༻

Prayer and Prophetic Word: Lord, I confess that I have not been yielded to you completely. I repent for the times you have wanted to use me for your purpose and I have been too busy with my own agenda. Lord, I give you all of who I am. I present myself as a living sacrifice to you for your purpose and pleasure. Take me and let me be a vessel of honor fit for your use. Discipline me. Mold me. Teach me. Lord, make me aware of the Holy Spirit living in me. I want the Holy Spirit to be a living reality in me. I submit to you, Holy Spirit. You can use me any way you want. I will be a vessel that you can use for your purposes. I say yes to you. In Jesus' name, I pray, amen and amen.

And I hear the Lord say: "I have been waiting for your 'Yes.' I have many things to give you, many wonders to show you. I want to use you as a vessel of honor. You will be one to bring great honor to me. You will be one to display my glory in a unique way. Thank you for saying 'Yes'. You could have said 'No' again, but you didn't. Now get ready for my 'Yes.'"

❧

Expressions of Worship

To worship God is to kiss Him. We kiss His heart, He kisses ours. Worship can take on many different forms, but I see two very different distinctions in the way we worship. These distinctions apply to every nationality, every tribe and tongue, and every person no matter their geographical location, race or gender.

The first form is an expression or expressions of worship. These are times we deliberately step out to praise, magnify, dance, or sing to the Lord. We might feel compelled to bow or to lie prostrate before Him. No matter what it looks and sounds like, the Lord loves it. He wants to hear our praise and adoration to Him. This expression can take place in our home, a corporate place of worship, a conference, or wherever we might be at the time. We might be alone, with a few, or in a crowd. This form of worship can bring freedom, change the atmosphere, break depression and anxiety, and cause us to get our eyes on Him, who is the answer to all things. Anyone can enter into this expression of worship.

While we have all probably expressed this worship at home, God wants us to worship corporately as well. He wants to break us out of containment, or any religious spirit that would keep us from being completely free in Him. Are you free in your corporate worship? He is worthy of our praise. It is for Him and Him alone. When we see the Lord for who He really is, we can't help but worship passionately and freely, without a thought of what others may think. If there are hindrances to your corporate worship, ask God to break you out of the fear of what others may think. Fear is a roadblock to freedom in worship.

There is a second form of worship that is greater than the first, and this type of worship requires a protocol. The kingdom of God is unlike any other kingdom in the world, with one exception; all kingdoms and cultures have their own set of rules or protocol that must be honored and followed. Webster's dictionary defines *protocol* as "customs and regulations dealing with diplomatic formality, precedence, and etiquette."

This second form of worship, which I will call lifestyle worship, is what the psalmist spoke about when he penned the words, "Worship the Lord in the beauty of holiness." (Psalm 29:2) What does it mean to worship the Lord in the beauty of holiness? To be holy does not mean we never sin, but it does mean we deliberately set ourselves apart from the "status quo" to be pleasing to Him and Him alone. This form of worship is a lifestyle. It requires being sensitive to the Holy Spirit and allowing Him to speak to us concerning our boundaries. It means to walk out our daily lives with an acute awareness of His presence with us. It is to know what pleases Him, and what doesn't, and being willing to say "no" to compromise in any situation or circumstance. This is the protocol of lifestyle worship.

If we were allowed access to the Queen of England, would we honor her? Of course we would. There would be specific protocol before, during and after our visit. In much the same way, the Holy Spirit is our diplomat, if you will, and will teach us the protocol of Father and Son. If we live in an attitude of worship and choose to walk in the Spirit we will know when we have quenched or grieved the Holy Spirit. If, or should I say when, that happens, we will know something is wrong and want to correct it immediately. We must become so sensitive to the Holy Spirit that we know when we are allowing Him to reign, and when we are not. The Holy Spirit will show us the correct protocol to bring the kingdom into any situation we are in. We are living in the end times that Jesus spoke about in the twenty-fourth chapter of Matthew. Lifestyle worship is a strategic key in these days and will be our greatest place of peace and safety. "For in Him we live and move and have our being." (Act 17:28)

In John 4:23 Jesus says, "But the hour is coming, and now is, when the true worshippers will worship the Father in spirit and truth; for the Father is seeking such to worship Him. God is Spirit, and those who worship Him must worship in spirit and truth." What are spirit and truth? To worship in spirit is to live and worship with the leading of Holy Spirit guiding our inner man. The Holy Spirit knows the Father perfectly, and He knows what pleases Father God. He will show us how to live in an attitude of worship. When we worship in truth, it is through Jesus. Jesus said in John 14:6, "I am the way, the truth, and the life. No one comes to the Father except through Me." And again in John 8:32, "…you shall know the truth, and the truth will set you free." When we worship in spirit and truth, there is freedom not to be compared to any other. Have you ever felt that kind of freedom? If so, then you were being led by the Holy Spirit. You were experiencing lifestyle worship, even though you may not have known how to define it. Lifestyle worship has no limits. It is not hindered by circumstances. It is "being," not "doing." To worship in spirit and truth is to worship in the oneness of the trinity. It is holiness (setting yourself apart), obedience, and most of all, being guided by the perfect love of the Father, the Son, and the Holy Spirit.

One final thought on worship. Break out of religious rules. Whether it is expressions of worship or lifestyle worship, don't allow a spirit of religion to keep you from full freedom. There were times Jesus broke the religious rules. He had to overturn tables twice in His earthly ministry, once at the beginning and then at the end. He did it because He knew who He was, and the authority He had from the Father. He was moving as the son of man fully yielded to the Holy Spirit, who knew the protocol of the kingdom. You can do that too, when you know who you are. Moving and living in the reality of who you are meant to be, breaks the spirit of the fear of man. I John 4:18 says, "There is no fear in love; but perfect love casts out fear, because fear involves torment..." If there is deep intimate love between you and the Lord, then perfect love can operate. The perfect love of the Father, the Son, and the Holy Spirit.

๑๖

Prayer and Declaration: Lord, teach me how to worship you in complete freedom. I confess and repent of the times I have been afraid to express my heartfelt love for you because of the fear of what others may think. Father, let your perfect love break any tormenting fear in my life, and let me be free to offer you the praise and worship you deserve. Lord, I want to live a worship lifestyle, set apart for your glory and purpose. I declare Lord, from this day forward I will bring you my worship, uninhibited by the fear of man or religious spirits. I declare, Lord, that my life will begin to portray lifestyle worship as I yield to the Holy Spirit's work in me. Thank you, Lord, for not giving up on me, but ever drawing me into your purpose and plan. In Jesus' name, I pray, amen and amen.

⊙✛⊙

Complete Surrender

What does complete surrender look like? It is yielding our whole life to Him for His purposes. Yielding our body, soul, and spirit. Yielding our plans, our hopes, our dreams and our future. It's easy when we experientially know the one we are yielding to. We know we can trust Him with anything. And we come to realize our greatest joy is His will for our lives. God says in Psalm 37:4, "Delight yourself also in the Lord, and He shall give you the desires of your heart." So why wouldn't we want to follow Him wholeheartedly? The Holy Spirit will show us, teach us and reveal the heart of the King to us.

Be abandoned to Him. Don't be afraid of letting Him in completely. He's a safe God. He knows us better than we know ourselves, because He's the one who created us. His heart is undone when we surrender to Him. Here is a secret that I have learned to experience Him: *Let time stand still in His presence.* Don't be in a hurry to leave because the time we give Him is a precious thing. When you come into His presence, leave everything else "at the door" and shut it behind you. It is just you and Him. Don't take the phone, the "to do" list, or the distractions. He's jealous over us. He wants time alone with us. He wants us focused on Him alone because His focus is on us. Song of Solomon 5:12 says, "His eyes are like doves…" That's focused eyes.

Total surrender will cost you. Don't be surprised if it looks different than you imagined. Sometimes Jesus broke the "religious rules" because of His total surrender to the Father, and sometimes we will have to break the man-made religious rules to demonstrate our complete commitment to God.

A beautiful example of total surrender is found in the book of John 12. This is the story of Mary of Bethany, the woman with the alabaster flask of very costly oil of spikenard. She was the one sitting at Jesus' feet every opportunity she had. There are three different places in the gospel that this story is recorded (Matthew 26:6-9; Mark 14:3-5; and John 12:1-3), but the Lord pointed me to the book of John. John was the disciple who had a very intimate relationship with Jesus and was known as the one Jesus loved: "Now there was leaning on Jesus' bosom one of His disciples, whom Jesus loved." (John 13:23) John tells the story of Mary of Bethany with a slightly different angle, which is his witness revealed by the Holy Spirit.

Mary had a special, intimate relationship with Jesus. Many times she was found lavishing her time on Him because of what He meant to her. Mary probably knew Him better than most. She brought Jesus her alabaster flask of very costly oil of spikenard. The root word for spikenard, or nard, in the Greek, is *pure*. It was very costly, not only because it was a valuable commodity in those days, but because it was costly and precious to *her. It represented all of her hopes, her dreams, and her very future.* It was something that couldn't be replaced. Imagine giving away, or pouring out something irreplaceable that represented your hope and future. Could you do it? John noticed and made note that in addition to anointing Jesus' head with it, which is an act of honor, she anointed His feet, which is an act of devotion. She was so devoted to Him and loved Him so, she was willing to give Him that which represented all of her hopes and dreams and her very future. This is a picture of total surrender. She literally poured out her future at His feet. She trusted Him and gave Him her all.

And then she wiped His feet with her hair. This was another act of extravagant devotion and humility. Suddenly, "…The house was filled with the fragrance of the oil." (John 12:3) This one act of pure devotion and surrender to Him caused a fragrant release of purity and love throughout the whole house. Her sacrificial gift, given in complete surrender, released the power of purity and love unlike anything else. *Selah.*

When she walked out of the house, the fragrance was in her hair and on her clothes, and she carried the power of that fragrant anointing wherever she went. Imagine that for a moment. She released purity and love wherever she went, and she never had to speak, pray, declare or decree a thing. The fragrance of that oil became the essence of who she was. It was a silent but powerful witness and declaration of who she had been with. "Now thanks be to God who always leads us in triumph in Christ, and through us diffuses the fragrance of His knowledge in every place." (2 Corinthians 2:14) It is the same for those who allow the Holy Spirit to have free reign in their lives. He gives us beauty preparations and fragrant oil. The Holy Spirit anoints us for the King and His service. This story of Mary and the alabaster flask is another great example of communication that goes beyond words. Bringing her expensive flask of oil spoke volumes to Jesus and others. And when she left the house, her fragrance spoke volumes without her having to utter a word. Her complete surrender was a testimony that affected many, and still does today.

In 2003, I had a dream that caused me to question my direction and ultimately to understand that I needed to surrender all. The dream began with the Lord mounted on a white horse looking down at me. He said, *"Are you ready to go?"* Even though the thought was exciting, I sensed the journey would be very long with a multitude of dangerous places along the way. Feeling the fear and apprehension, I said no. He paused a moment, looked intently at me, and then slowly and reluctantly, turned and called out to someone else to come. That person mounted the horse with Him, and they rode off. As I stood there watching them disappear into the distance, I thought about some of the dangers they would encounter. There would be falling rocks, wide crevices in the land, wild animals, and treacherous rivers to cross. I imagined an arduous, dangerous journey. After a while I realized I didn't want to stay where I was, even if it meant danger. So with everything within me, I shouted at the top of my lungs, hoping He would hear me: "Wait! I want to come!"

Suddenly He was right there in front of me, smiling as if He were very pleased. He said, "You have to change your clothes. Which one do you want?" I looked down to where He pointed, at the two garments on the ground that had mysteriously appeared. The first looked like a gypsy outfit. It was very colorful and looking at it gave me a sense of freedom. But the longer I looked, it began to evoke a feeling of loneliness and sadness to me. It seemed to depict a life of aimless wandering. I then turned my eyes to the second garment, and the beauty of it literally took my breath away. It was the most beautiful wedding dress I had ever seen. Brilliantly white and glistening so much I had to shield my eyes to look at it. It seemed to radiate with purity, and I felt such joy just looking at it. There was no doubt in my mind which garment I would choose. The dress was beautiful and made me feel like I could conquer the world. I was delighted! Then I woke up.

I asked the Lord about this dream, and He directed me to Revelation 19:7 "…the marriage of the Lamb has come, and His wife has made herself ready." and Rev 22:17, "And the Spirit and the Bride say "'Come!'" I understood several things from that dream and the interpretation the Lord gave.

First of all, I understood I had a certain amount of fear associated with being wholehearted for the Lord, and His calling to complete surrender. I also understood in spite of the fear, I didn't want to stay where I was. And lastly, I understood that to go where He is calling meant a change in the way I see myself. In the dream, I had to make a choice about the clothes I would wear in the next season, in my journey with Him. Would I continue to wander aimlessly, or would I decide to follow Him wholeheartedly, in complete surrender, where He would lead me?

Have you ever been in a similar situation? Knowing you are being pulled two different ways? As Christians, this is not an uncommon thing for us. But the fact is we can no longer put off decisions that we could in the past. We are now on God's timetable and must make a choice. The Lord is requiring complete obedience if we are to partner with Him for these end times. The plumb line has dropped and the countdown has begun. Are we going to let go of our fears and doubts and trust Him with all that is in us? Are we ready to be wholeheartedly His? The scripture He gave in Revelation 19:7 states the marriage has come and the bride has made herself ready. In other words, the time of preparation is over. The time is now. It is God's appointed time for the bride to be fully revealed and take her place by her bridegroom. She has been preparing herself but *now* is the time to embrace her new identity. The new identity has a new authority, given by God Himself, and facilitated by the Holy Spirit.

Are you ready for the journey? Have you made yourself ready? We have our part of getting ready, and He has His part in preparing us. It all works together for His greater purpose and glory. As His bride, we are an extension of Him. We have His heart, His mind, His thoughts, His desires and feelings, and His agenda. What an honor! God's ultimate desire is to have a bride for His son Jesus. One who will work alongside Him, and partner with Him. A bride who will be one with Father, Son, and Holy Spirit; working and reigning together. That, my beloved, is complete surrender. And just a reminder once again: the bride is not about gender, but a position of authority reserved for those who wholeheartedly say "Yes."

৩৳৩

Prayer and Declaration: Lord, I am beginning to understand the benefits of complete surrender. But Lord, I don't know if I am capable of that. I ask you to help me to surrender completely to you and your will for my life. Forgive me for the times I've taken things into my own hands, thinking I knew better than you. Forgive me for the times I have run ahead of you, and times I have lagged behind in my complacency. Help me, Lord, to be a willing vessel that you can work through, wherever and whenever you desire. Thank you, Lord, that you are calling me to take my place as the bride of Christ, to stand in the authority that you have given me. I pray to always walk before you in a spirit of humility, seeking to please only you. Thank you for your Holy Spirit who will help me on the journey. Lord, I declare that I am willing to walk in complete surrender to you. I declare that my life will be not only a silent witness, but I will speak of your love every opportunity I am given. I thank you that right now, you are drawing others, and confirming your desires in their lives as well. Father, I declare there will be a clear recognition of the new mantles and callings you are passing out; the larger anointing that will expand our territory. I decree a spirit of wisdom and understanding is being released to us now. I decree we are dressed for battle and will operate in everything you have given us. Thank you, Lord, for the warrior bride anointing, the Esther anointing, for such a time as this. In your precious mighty name, Jesus, amen and amen.

ᴓᴦᴓ

His Ultimate Desire

In John 17:21-23 Jesus prays,

> ...that they all may be one, as you, Father, are in Me and I in you; that they also may be one in Us, that the

world may believe that you sent Me. And the glory which you gave Me I have given them, that they may be one just as We are one: I in them, and you in Me; that they may be made perfect in one, and that the world may know that you have sent Me, and have loved them as you have loved Me.

What a powerful prayer! Jesus goes on to say in verse 24, "Father, I desire that they also whom you gave Me may be with Me where I am, that they may behold My glory which you have given Me…" This is one of the most powerful and intimate prayers that Jesus ever prayed. This prayer was not only His desire but the Father's heart. We don't really know where Father "ends" and Jesus "begins," and vice versa. But one thing is sure: From this prayer, we know we will ultimately be one with the Godhead and experience the glory of the Holy Triune.

Do you recognize where He ends and you begin? Ponder this question for a moment. To be one with Him is our ultimate goal. But not only is it our goal, it is His ultimate desire. So we can be sure the Father will answer this prayer, as we are willing to yield to His purpose and work in us. As His bride, we are to be an extension of Him. That means one with Him, part of Him, and extended from Him. His thoughts, His feelings, His words, and His power all flowing down through us. When this becomes a reality in our lives, then we have truly become one with Him.

In April of 2006, the Lord gave me an experience of becoming one with Him. While it is difficult to explain this experience, I believe it was a transitory state in which the Lord opened a portal into heaven and allowed me to experience something very supernatural. In my secret place with the Lord, I was pleading to be one with Him, literally consumed in Him, that we would truly be one in spirit. Suddenly, I had the sensation of becoming a liquid vapor; a liquid essence. In that state, I saw Jesus in the same way, and we began to be intermingled, just as you would see vapor or steam rising and intermingling. I felt as if my spirit was becoming a part of His spirit, and I sensed that our spirits were communing and dancing. At one point, I actually felt consumed in Him, and then I heard the Lord speak, "…Therefore what God has joined together, let not man separate." (Matthew 19:6) That scripture speaks of a man and woman being joined together in marriage, in holy matrimony; No longer two, but one. I understood by that experience, plus the word God spoke, that is exactly what He wants. He wants to be one with us, just as He and the Lord and Holy Spirit are one. He wants a holy covenant joining us. He wants to know we are His as much as He is ours. That is intimacy on the deepest level.

ᛜ

Prayer, Declaration, and Prophetic Word: OK, Lord. Forgive me for trying to figure it out without consulting you in the process. I trust you. I will be yours alone, submitted and yielded to you. I wait for you. I wait on you. I decree and come into agreement with your prayer that we become one. I want to be an extension of you, Lord. Please make us one. Just as you grant my heart's desire, Lord, let me grant your heart's desire to be one. I decree that my heart will be completely surrendered to you. In Jesus' precious mighty name, I pray, amen and amen.

And I hear the Lord saying, "Don't try to be 'anything,' just be mine. As you wholeheartedly give yourself to me, I will direct your steps. I will show you where, I will show you how, I will show you when, and I will show you what. That is enough for you to know now."

๑๖

Reflections on Chapter Three

1. How do you plan to incorporate foundational obedience into your lifestyle?

_____

_____

_____

_____

_____

_____

_____

_____

2. List the areas you want your trust in God to grow. Explain in detail how you will get there.

_____

_____

_____

_____

_____

_____

_____

_____

_____

3. What is lifestyle worship and how can you improve yours?
Be specific.

_____

_____

_____

_____

_____

_____

_____

_____

_____

CHAPTER 4

The Passion that Produces Power

Have you ever been really passionate about something? Is your passion to sing or dance? Is it to paint or write? Or maybe your passion is not so much about doing something as it is to have something in particular; a special car, or home, or maybe a business. Your passion could be for a person, maybe your spouse, or for a baby. Whatever your passion might be, it creates an excitement in your heart. It infuses you with eagerness and joy and gives an added zeal to your life. There is power in passion.

God created us to have desires and passions in our life. God has given us all things to enjoy, but none of them should take preeminence in our heart over Him. God wants our passion to be first and foremost for Him. His passion for us is focused and intent. He is a jealous God, and He will stop at nothing to make sure our heart priorities are in order. "For you shall worship no other god, for the Lord, whose name is Jealous, is a jealous God." (Exodus 34:14)

Understanding the depths of God's desire for us produces a desire for Him. It's true. God created us that way. When we are loved with unconditional love, we can't help but love back. Combined passion (His for us and ours for Him) produces exponential power. It causes us to be bold, to step out and do things we wouldn't ordinarily do. There is power in love. A person in love cannot be talked out of it. They cannot be reasoned out of it, and they cannot deny it.

Love will make us do crazy things sometimes. God's love for us is crazy like that. He loved us so much that He sent His only Son to die for us. That's pretty radical, don't you think? That's the ultimate sacrifice, to give the one you love with all heart and soul. There was power in that sacrificial act of giving. And look at the love of Jesus. He loved His Father unconditionally, and He wanted His bride so much, that He was *willing* to die for us. When He was hanging on the cross, the Bible says, "And Jesus cried out again with a loud voice, and yielded up His spirit." (Matthew 27:50) He was willing to do whatever it took to reconcile us to Himself and to the Father. How hard that must have been for Him to be separated from His Father and Holy Spirit! He had been with them since the beginning of time. He had never experienced separation from either of them but knew it was all for a higher plan. That is love in action. His passion and love produced great power that could not be denied. Matthew 27:51-54 states,

> Then, behold, the veil of the temple was torn in two from top to bottom; and the earth quaked, and the rocks were split, and the graves were opened; and many bodies of the saints who had fallen asleep were raised; and coming out of the graves after His resurrection, they went into the holy city and appeared to many. So when the centurion and those with him, who were guarding Jesus, saw the earthquake and the things that had happened, they feared greatly saying, 'Truly this was the Son of God!'

This kind of all-encompassing love demanded a response.

The Holy Spirit was part of this divine plan also. The Holy Spirit knew there would come a time when He would leave His beloved Jesus: *"Father, into your hands I commit My spirit."* (Luke 23:46) The Holy Spirit had been with Jesus since the beginning, but He knew there was a time coming. He knew the plan and was part of it. He agreed to depart from the One He loved with all of His heart so a greater purpose could be accomplished. Again, that was a passion that produced power. Listen; when we give up our rights to ourselves for the higher purposes of God, it produces power! God sees the passion in our hearts to be obedient, and when we act out of obedience, power is released. This is power that advances the kingdom and annihilates the darkness. The Holy Spirit chose to follow the plan of the Father: the power it produced came forth in the resurrection of Jesus, then again with the hundred and twenty in the upper room and from there to the uttermost parts of the earth. It was not only a geographical power that spread, but a timeless power that continues to this day and that grows stronger and greater with the passing of time.

The passion that produces power is very real and ever increasing. It is exponential because you cannot kill love. It is ever expanding. Love never fails, it will never become obsolete. It is a force so powerful that nothing can stop it. This kind of passion was of Father, Son, and Holy Spirit since before time. It is a commodity of the Kingdom. Isaiah 9:7 says, "Of the increase of His government [kingdom] and peace there will be no end..."

Let's look at another example in scripture of love and passion that produced incredible power. There was a love that drew Jesus' heart to the point that He had to respond. As the story unfolds in the book of John, chapter nineteen, Jesus was crucified and buried. The story continues in chapter twenty: "Now the first day of the week Mary Magdalene went to the tomb early, while it was still dark..." (John 20:1) She was the first one there. Her love for Him compelled her to go to the tomb. She needed to be close to Him.

> But Mary stood outside by the tomb weeping; and as she wept she stooped down and looked into the tomb. And she saw two angels in white sitting, one at the head and the other at the foot, where the body of Jesus had lain. Then they said to her, "Woman, why are you weeping?" She said to them, "Because they have taken away my Lord, and I do not know where they have laid Him." Now when she had said this she turned around and saw Jesus standing there, and did not know that it was Jesus. Jesus said to her, "Woman, why are you weeping? Whom are you seeking?" She, supposing Him to be the gardener, said to Him, "Sir, if you have carried Him away, tell me where you have laid Him, and I will take Him away." Jesus turned to her and said "Mary!"
>
> John 20:11-16

And when He said her name, she recognized Him. She knew His voice. She was the first at the tomb, and she was last at the tomb. The love she had for Him drew her. For all practical intents and purposes, He was gone; dead and buried. But while His love drew her, at the same time, her love was drawing Him. It drew Him so much so, that He made a detour on His way to ascend to His Father. "Do not cling to Me, for I have not yet ascended to My Father; but go to My brethren and say to them, 'I am ascending to My Father, and to My God and your God.'" (John 20:17) Can you imagine how Jesus felt at that moment? Here was a woman who displayed such love for Him; not only was she first and last at the tomb, but her intention was to be with Him wherever He was, as we see when she cried out to know where His missing body lay. That act of devotion and passion delighted and probably even humbled Jesus' heart, seeing how she cared for Him. And it bears repeating. Her love drew Him; So much so that He took a detour before ascending to the Father, and revealed Himself to her. Jesus chose Mary, the one whom He had cast demons out of, to be the one to take the message of His resurrection to His disciples. And the reality of His resurrection was revealed to her first, because she drew Him with her relentless love. That, my friend, is the passion that produces power. Just as she drew Him, it is possible for us to draw Him. Indeed, love demands a response.

Was It All in Vain?

It was January 2005, and I was at a *'Starting the Year Off Right'* conference in Denton, Texas, facilitated by Apostle Chuck Pierce. While asleep in my hotel room, the Lord gave me a powerful dream that impacted me tremendously. I have remembered it at very strategic times in my life because it is a key, not only to my moving forward in Him, but for the entire body and bride of Christ to move forward as well.

In the dream, we were actually at the final session of the conference. I saw myself and many others walking out of the building with our arms stacked high with gift packages, each one beautifully wrapped. The packages represented anointings, revelations, and spiritual gifts that God had given us to be able to walk in complete victory, power and authority in the days and months ahead. But when we walked through and out the doors, we tossed the gifts down. We were still "talking" about them, but we weren't "using" them. We had tossed them aside. We were all excited about what we had just received, but ironically, we weren't going to use and manifest what God had given. Suddenly, I felt the grief in the Lord's heart and I heard Him say, "Was it all in vain?" I saw Jesus hanging on the cross, pierced and bleeding, and then I heard the scripture, "But He was wounded for our transgressions, He was bruised for our iniquities; the chastisement of our peace was upon Him, and by His stripes we are healed." (Isaiah 53:5) I saw myself standing at the foot of the cross looking up at His broken, bleeding body. Then again I heard Him say, "Was it all in vain?" Suddenly my heart was broken in grief and repentance because I had tossed aside the precious gifts He had given. The things that had cost Him so dearly, and what He had wanted to give us so desperately, had been taken so lightly. The value of what He had done was of little worth as we threw down the gifts He had given. Needless to say, I awoke from that dream with a deep sense of sadness and grief, realizing what the Lord was communicating to me. I still remember the look in His eyes when He asked me, "Was it all in vain?" He paid a great price to redeem us. He also paid a great price for us to walk in freedom and victory in every area of our lives. He paid for our redemption, and then He freely gave us the tools we need to live a victorious life.

That dream had such an impact on my life. I determined from that point on, to the best of my ability, to step out and use the gifts the Lord has given me. What about you? What have we got to lose? He's already paid it all! His one act of selfless love paved the way for our victory. This is the power of love, His unconditional love. He only asks that we take it and use it.

What gifts has God given you? Are there any you are aware of that you've laid down and are not using? Some gifts He gives to all of us as a corporate body, such as the five-fold ministry gifts Paul speaks about in Ephesians 4:11-13. These are the offices of the apostle, the prophet, the evangelist, the pastor and the teacher. Then there are gifts of the manifestation of the Spirit that we grow into, as we mature. These are found in I Corinthians 12:8-11. They are the word of wisdom, the word of knowledge, faith, gifts of healings, the working of miracles, prophecy, discerning of spirits, different kinds of tongues, and the interpretation of tongues. These can also be given by God instantaneously at His will. There are several other gifts mentioned such as the gift of exhortation, administration, help, and giving. Then we have natural gifts that we are born with. They are usually things we love to do and are naturally good at. Is yours a creative gift to draw, paint, sing, dance, or work with your hands? Is it a gift to speak, or to know how to bring people together for a specific cause? Whatever gifts God has given us, let's use them to the best of our ability to bring Him honor.

☙

Prayer and Declaration: I confess Lord, that there have been times I have not used my gifts, either out of fear, pride, complacency, or just not loving enough. Forgive me, Lord, for my negligence and carelessness in this area. You paid too great a price for me to neglect my gifts. I declare Lord, from this day forward, I will use my gifts to the best of my ability to bring glory to your name. You said Lord, to whom much is given much is required. I know, Lord, that you have given me much. I declare from this day forward I will accept and walk in the responsibility that you have given me to use my gifts. I declare as I use my gifts, others will be edified and many will be brought to the Kingdom through my gifts being activated. And I decree, Lord, that you will receive the honor you deserve from my life. In Jesus' mighty name, amen and amen.

☙

The Place of Absolute Love

The following is an excerpt taken from the book *Secrets of the Secret Place* by Bob Sorge:

Many people see the cross as a place of pain and restriction, and that is true. But it is so much more! The cross is the place of absolute love. The cross is the Father saying to the world, "This is how much I love you!" The cross is the Son saying to the Father, "This is how much I love you!" And the cross is the bride saying to her bridegroom, "This is how much I love you!" The cross is consummate passion poured forth. When Christ calls us to share His cross, He invites us to the highest intimacy. The wood that holds His hands now holds our hands. The nail that binds His feet to the will of God crisscrosses the nail that impales our feet to that same will. Here we hang, two lovers on opposite sides of one cross, our hearts almost touching except for the separating wood. This is our marriage bed. "Here I give to thee my love."

This is the passion that produces power!

To really know Him, we must live on both sides of the cross. One side is the place of death to self for a greater purpose; the other side is the resurrection power produced from embracing death to self. It takes both sides of the cross to really know Him, to become intimately acquainted with Him. This is what Paul talked about in Philippians 3:10: "That I may know Him and the power of His resurrection, and the fellowship of His sufferings, being conformed to His death ..."

We cannot have one without the other. Death to self cannot be attained until we first know Him but once we know Him, we are able to embrace that death. After death comes resurrection, and after resurrection comes higher ascension; then the cycle continues with death to another part of ourselves. We can choose to stay at any level we want, but in order to really know Him, to continuously live and move and have our being in Him, we must embrace the *process*. It is the process of death and resurrection that produces a passion for Him, and ultimately power through Him. Our intimacy with God paves the way to be able to die to selfish desires, and then, the resurrection will bring new understanding, wisdom, and power; but beloved, there is always more. And because He wants more of us, He will allow us to once again be brought to the place where we make a choice to give up our right to ourselves. I hear the Lord saying to us, *"Do you want more of Me? Then give Me more of you."*

Opening our hearts to God's love is the answer to everything we need. I had a dream several years ago about a precious couple that I am friends with. In the dream, I saw two large root balls, much like you would see if you pulled a tree out of the ground by the roots. I asked the Lord about these two root balls and He told me they were the roots of bitterness. I remembered the scripture in Hebrew 12:15: "Look after each other so that not one of you will fail to find God's best blessings. Watch out that no bitterness takes root among you, for as it springs up it causes deep trouble, hurting many in their spiritual lives."(The Living Bible) I discerned that because of circumstances, hurt, and rejection in the lives of these two, bitterness had taken root. I was praying about this when I heard Him say, *"I have the antidote. It is love – My love."* He then directed me to Ephesians 3:17-19:

> ...May your roots go down deep into the soil of God's marvelous love; and may you be able to feel and understand, as all God's children should, how long, how wide, how deep and how high His love really is; and to experience for yourselves, though it is so great that you will never see the end of it or fully know or understand it. And so at last you will be filled up with God Himself
>
> The Living Bible

Love is the answer; love never fails. No matter what situation or circumstance you are facing, the pure unconditional love of God is the answer. When His unconditional love draws our hearts, it is more powerful than any spoken or unspoken prayer. Yes, His love is greater than any prayer, any declaration, any miracle, or any Bible study. Mike Bickle, in his study on the *Song of Solomon*, writes, "Lovesickness for Jesus will be the most powerful and most mysterious reality in all the world at the end of the age. It will have the strongest drawing power both to believers and unbelievers. It will be more powerful than apostolic wisdom or miracles." *Selah*. Can you imagine? There is a love that defies all logic and reasoning. It is stronger than any sign or wonder. This love will have a greater drawing power than anything we have ever known. And this love, my friend, is what we are being prepared to receive and walk in. If I didn't have that witness in my spirit, I would say it is almost too good to be true. But it is true!

∞

Prayer and Declaration: Lord, I am willing to go through the process of death and resurrection to know you more. I pray, like Paul, that I may know you, the power of your resurrection, and the fellowship of your sufferings. I want to know you in all your completeness. I know love is the answer to everything. Create in me a passionate love for you that will produce resurrection living, not only in me, but through me to a dying world. I know it takes God to love God, and so I am asking for more of you in my life. Lord, my love has been too small. Enlarge my capacity to love you and others. I decree, Lord, that I will position myself to receive your love. I decree that any hindrance to receiving the fullness of your love will be removed from my life. And Father, I declare that the love you impart to me will have the same power as when you imparted it to Jesus. In His precious name I pray, amen and amen.

∞

The Passion that Creates a Flow

I was once again in the secret place, pressing into the Lord and giving Him all of my heart. I had been feeling for a couple of weeks that my heart had been divided, with so many things going on and being pulled here and there. But I knew at this moment my heart was completely His again. His presence was so strong all I could do was weep and tell Him how much I loved Him.

Suddenly I began to smell His fragrance. It came in waves like the ocean tide. I could smell His sweet scent very distinctly, and then it would ebb. This happened several times, and I eventually realized the aroma was a combination of frankincense and myrrh. I have anointing oil made from the two, and I recognized the fragrance. I suddenly had a vision of Him leaning over and interceding for me. It was so real; I felt His tangible love like a thick honey being poured over me. As the aroma of frankincense flowed in once again, I knew His intercession was being poured out. I could literally feel it, along with His love. Then as the aroma of frankincense ebbed out and the fragrance of myrrh came flowing in, I felt His obedience unto death in my very being. He was allowing me to feel just a portion of what He was feeling. At the same time, I knew He was feeling my obedience to die to the things that had been pulling my heart from His. I was feeling His pain and passion and He was feeling mine.

The Holy Spirit then dropped this scripture into my spirit: "that I may know Him and the power of His resurrection, and the fellowship of His sufferings, being conformed to His death..." (Philippians 3:10) Then I understood what was happening: He was allowing me to share in the fellowship of His sufferings. It was such an incredible experience; feeling the pain and passion of one another; and all the while knowing He was praying for me in it and through it. This experience left an indelible mark upon my heart. It caused me to know, without a doubt, that He knows right where we are, and He is interceding for us to make it through to the end.

Experiences like this will create lovesickness in your life, and a life of lovesickness creates a flow in the Holy Spirit. When we move as one with Jesus and experience His life, creativity is produced. Life becomes a flow of Holy Spirit. And in that flow, there is not only creativity, but there is a sense of purpose and power. The flow of the Holy Spirit creates a life that is fun and exciting. When people see our vitality and love for Jesus, it will cause them to hunger for what we have. They will see a reality in our lives that is not in theirs, and it will create holy jealousy (or envy). This holy jealousy will cause them to cry out to know Him. Listen, love begets love. When you observe a person in love, their whole countenance radiates with joy. They walk in an atmosphere of life and excitement. People are looking for experiential love. And the wonderful thing is that anyone can have it if they know Jesus in a deep, holy, intimate way. Falling in love with Him is easy when you know the wonders of all that He is.

The Song of Solomon is an allegorical story of the love and life of our bridegroom King Jesus, and His beloved bride, which is us. To summarize the story, there are many experiences and emotions they go through, but through it all, their passionate love grows and matures, and creates a flow of love wherever they go. In Song of Solomon 5:10, the bride answers the question given by those around her, "Why are you so crazy about Him?" With undeniable passion, she explains His attributes, His beauty, and His majesty. In fact, she explains Him so well that they get it! They finally understand why she is so in love with Him. And they realize they want what she has. They want to know Him the way she does. " ... Where has your beloved turned aside, that we may seek Him with you?" (Song of Solomon 6:1) There is a passion that produces power. Would you like to influence believers and non-believers alike to know Him in a deep way? The passion and love you carry for Him can be seen, felt, and heard in everything you do. This love is transferable from Him, through you, and out to others. Allow the glory of the Lord, and His countenance, to shine through you. His glory and your passion draw the hearts of others to want to know Him more. It creates a flow that is captivating and undeniable.

❧

Prayer and Declaration: Lord Jesus, I pray to love you with my whole heart. I want my life to be a living witness that draws others to you, and I ask that my passion for you be so undeniable that it causes others to want what I have in you. Lord, I declare that my life will be a continuous flow of holy passion that changes the atmosphere wherever I go. I decree that my life will be a flow of your holy love, Lord. One that will produce power to change lives and hearts. I decree that your love flowing through me will melt hearts in this hour. And I declare, Lord, that my life will be an extension of yours, bringing glory to you alone. In Jesus' name I pray, amen and amen.

❧

The Bride Moving in Authority

Have you ever seen someone who exudes confidence and assurance? Someone who isn't afraid to step up and speak out? There have been times I've been in a room with others, or in a gathering, and someone comes in who carries themselves in such a way that people can't help but notice. That person may not necessarily be the best dressed or even exceptionally good looking by the world's standards, but something about them draws you. That "something" is the confidence of knowing who they are, and where they are going. They exude magnetism that you can't help but be attracted to. This magnetism is like a rod of authority. It is like Aaron's rod that budded, showing the one God had granted authority.

The person I am describing is the bride of Christ moving in authority. She knows who she is and whose she is. She knows her purpose and where she's going. It bears repeating here again, that the bride of Christ is not about gender, but it's about a position. It is about a person, male or female, knowing the position they hold and moving in the authority of that position. As the bride of Christ, our agenda is our bridegroom's agenda. As we carry out His plans, He gives us the authority needed to complete our assignment.

When we move in His authority, things around us will change. Atmospheres clear, miracles manifest, the enemy has to bow, and the Lord is glorified. Let's consider Esther again in her position as queen. She knew the authority she had as the bride, and she stepped out in that authority to save her people from destruction. Esther 5:1 says, "Now it happened on the third day that Esther put on her royal robes and stood in the inner court of the king's palace..." The fact that it was the third day represented the perfect timing of Father God. The royal robes represented her authority or the covenant she had with the King; and the inner court, where she stood, represented the relationship and intimacy she had with Him.

Like Queen Esther, we as the bride of Christ are standing at the same threshold right now. We are in God's timing for a manifestation of the sons and daughters of God. As the world grows darker, His glory is burning brighter in His bride. We have been clothed with His authority because of our covenant with Him, and we know (yada) Him. Like Queen Esther, it is the third day, we have on our royal robes, and we are standing in the inner court. We are about to see the manifestation of our relationship and authority.

There is one very important fact to note concerning the bride moving in authority. We became the bride because of covenant and intimacy, and we will advance in authority by covenant and intimacy. We must never lose the understanding of what it takes to be the bride. Covenant and intimacy will continue to move us forward. The Word says, "… Perfect love casts out fear …." (1 John 4:18) As we understand our covenant through intimacy with Him, it will cause us to be bold and courageous. Fear and confusion will not hinder our advancement. To illustrate this truth, the Lord gave me a vision in September of 2007. This vision has impacted me greatly through the years, and still does today. I know it is not just to teach and encourage me, but it is for the whole body of Christ.

I had been in intercession during the very early hours of the morning and laid down at 5:00 a.m. I immediately had a dream that lasted for fifteen minutes and then I woke. In the dream, I was in a jeep with no top on it, and sitting at the base of a mountain. Looking up the mountain, I saw dangerous terrain, large jutting rocks, wide crevices, and steep inclines that seemed impossible to navigate. The Lord was in the back seat of the jeep, and He leaned forward, and put His hands over my eyes, and said, *"Now GO!"* We started laughing; it was scary and exciting at the same time.

I began to drive up the mountain with His hands covering my eyes. I had the distinct impression I was seeing with His eyes, hearing with His ears, and understanding what He was thinking. I was operating with His mind, the mind of Christ. I was literally navigating the jeep up the mountain and around all the danger, not having any of my own faculties to work with. The whole time, we were both laughing and having a great time! It was so much fun and so exhilarating! The further we went, the more I was able to trust Him and His direction, even though in the natural realm I could not see. And interestingly, He was not speaking directions out loud to me; I was hearing Him by the Spirit , and sensing things the same way.

What I was experiencing was a higher form of communication. It was Spirit to spirit. I believe this higher form of communication will begin to be the norm for the bride of Christ. As communication lines advance in the natural realm, so God will increase the ability for us to communicate by His Spirit. Spirit communication is a strategic weapon of warfare, unlike anything we have experienced, or unlike anything the enemy can know or understand.

At one point we stopped, and I opened my eyes and saw two very small people, similar to midgets, standing in front of the jeep. One was very ominous and mean looking, and the other was "jabbering" things I didn't understand. I said to the Lord "What is he saying?" and then I asked, "Lord, who are they?" He said, "Fear and confusion." I turned and looked at them again; they seemed so small and insignificant. I said, "*This* is fear and confusion!?" As soon as I said it, they began to tremble and back away, and then turned and ran.

I realized they were afraid of me. Then I understood it was because I was operating in Him; His eyes, His ears, and His mind. Then the dream ended. When I woke, the scripture the Lord dropped in my spirit was Acts 17:28: "In Him we live, and move, and have our being." Wow!

This dream is a perfect example of the bride of Christ moving in authority. It is all about Him. We become an extension of Him in every way.

∞

Prayer, Declaration, and Prophetic Word: Lord, I pray to move as a perfect extension of you. I pray to live and move and have my being in you. Lord, I know as I commune and spend time with you, you will teach me many things. I want to come to a place where I see what you see, hear what you hear, and do what you do. I want every move I make to be with you. Every thought yours, Lord. I want to be your bride moving in authority and intimacy. I want to radiate your glory. Lord, I decree and declare, I will live, and move, and have my being in you. In Jesus' name I pray, amen and amen.

And I hear the Lord saying to us, "Because you have asked in accordance with my will and my desires, what you ask will be granted. Even now I am granting. Step out of the place of familiarity and into the place of freshness; then you will begin to experience Spirit to spirit transmission. It is the language of the heart."

Reflections on Chapter Four

1. What is your passion in life? How can you use your passion to glorify God?

_____

_____

_____

_____

_____

_____

_____

2. What gifts has God given you that you're not yet using? How do you plan to implement those gifts?

_____

_____

_____

_____

_____

_____

_____

3. What do you feel is holding you back from the place of authority that God has given you as the bride of Christ? What mindset must be changed in order for you to move forward?

_____

_____

_____

_____

_____

_____

_____

_____

_____

CHAPTER 5

Corporate Intimacy— Fact or Fiction

We all know there is intimacy in the "secret place," the inner chamber where it's just you and Him. In that setting, He is very real and undeniable. The question is, can there be such a place in the corporate church setting? And if so, how does that work? What does it look like? How does it feel? To answer these questions, we must get out of our own mindsets, and think from the mind of Christ. How does He feel about corporate intimacy? God's ways are not our ways, His thoughts not ours. To understand this, we must not allow traditions and "the way we've always done it" to have precedence over His desires. Neither can we allow the fear of what others may think to control our actions when it comes to Him. Luke chapter seven tells the story of the woman who poured the fragrant oil on Jesus' feet in the house of the Pharisee. She broke religious rules to display her love. We too, must come to a place where loving Him is the greatest thing in our lives, and because of our love, we care more about showing Him that love than being concerned how it looks to others.

How do we know His desires concerning corporate intimacy? Let's take a look at what His word says, which always provides a foundation of truth in our search for Him. In scripture, the word "corporate" is not used. In its place is the word gather, gathered, or gathering. It's where believers meet together. In essence, it means the same as corporate. It is a gathering together in one place, a unity, an assembling, or a congregation. "And let them make Me a sanctuary that I may dwell among them." (Exodus 25:8) God wants to dwell among His gathered people. He wants fellowship with us in the corporate place. He wants to dwell in His sanctuary; to live, abide, rest, remain and make His home among His people.

When God finds a corporate people who will allow Him to abide and remain, His very presence commands a response from us. And that response is not a church program or a religious ceremony. He's looking for a heart to heart connection. "But the hour is coming, and now is, when the true worshippers shall worship the Father in spirit and truth; for the Father is seeking such to worship Him."(John 4:23)

We do not want to miss the mark in our corporate worship by allowing a program to take the place of heart to heart connection. God loved the tabernacle of David because the veil that had separated Him from the people was pulled back for all the people to enter His presence, and dwell once again with Him. Their response to His presence was twenty-four-hour praise and worship in the beauty of holiness. In the book of Acts, after the Holy Spirit came, James stood up and declared to the people the words of Amos 9:11: "On that day [the appointed time] I will raise up the tabernacle of David, which has fallen down, and repair its damages; I will raise up its ruins, and rebuild it as in the days of old." This is a prophetic promise that God will have the corporate heart-to-heart intimacy He desires.

When God looks down from heaven onto a corporate body that loves and worships Him in spirit and truth, with eyes and hearts focused on Him alone, I can only imagine what He must feel. Oh, the power of corporate love and oneness! It touches His heart in a way that He can't help but release His will into the earth. When God finds a "gathered" body that will come in agreement with Him, and press in to know His heart, that body becomes a breeding ground for miracles. This is the place He delights to release His heart and His hand.

In a corporate gathering, you can actually prepare the atmosphere for His presence to be welcome. That would include things like music and lighting. In the natural realm, just as you "set the mood" for time alone with the one you love, you can do the same corporately. He is more than willing. There have been times in corporate praise and worship where I have felt a literal change in the atmosphere and knew He was calling us all into a deeper place with Him. Eyes close, hearts open, hands raise, and knees bow … it's a natural response to the One that has just entered and revealed Himself. Then the divine exchange of love begins – the drawing of the Lord to each one of us. It is at this point that we experience openings, or portals, into the glory realm. The glory realm causes what has been in the invisible realm to invade the visible. God reveals His love to us because we have revealed our love to Him.

When we move into the place of God's rest in the corporate setting, the Holy Spirit teaches us how to respond to His presence and receive His impartation. In the atmosphere of corporate rest, it is very easy to receive from God. It might be physical or emotional healing, peace, strength, gifts of His spirit, or His very own glorious nature. Jesus is praying for all believers,

> … that they all may be one, as you, Father, are in Me, and I in you; that they also may be one in Us, that the world may believe that you sent Me. And the glory which you gave Me I have given them, that they may be one just as We are one: I in them and you in Me;

that they may be made perfect in one, and that the world may know that you have sent Me, and have loved them as you have loved Me.

John 17:21-23

Let's explore the different aspects of the corporate anointing. God's house should always feel like Him, sound like Him and reveal His character. His house will have a spiritual fragrance. A house where He is Lord will personify freedom, because He is a God of freedom. "Now the Lord is the Spirit; and where the Spirit of the Lord is, there is liberty." (2 Corinthians 3:17) There will be worship and intercession mingled together. There will be instruments and dance. We will experience weeping and laughing. There will be people lying prostrate, and others jumping for joy. It can look rather "messy" and possibly undesirable and offensive to religious spirits. But all of these different forms of worship will release the glory of God, where miracles, signs, wonders, and healings abound. Don't be afraid to let God be God, and move with the Holy Spirit. The more you know Him, the easier it is to let go of any hindering fears and let Him dwell first of all in your house (the temple of your body), and then in His corporate house.

❦

Prayer and Declaration: Father, forgive us for the times we have met corporately and had no expectation of your presence. We repent for "settling" into a form of worship that has grieved your heart and kept you at a distance. Lord, would you release upon us and through us the passion and power of the Holy Spirit to ignite our hearts for you and you alone? Lord, we declare from this day forward that as we enter into corporate worship, it will be with our hearts and minds focused on you alone. Lord, we declare we will be a corporate people of true worshippers. And Father, we declare as we lay down our programs and enter into true worship, it will cause you to release your love and power in a greater measure. Thank you, Lord, for the realization that everything we need is in you. You ARE the answer. In Jesus' name I pray, amen and amen.

Dwelling in Unity

In Genesis v.11, the people began to build a tower at Babel, one that would reach to the high heavens. Their reason for building the tower was to make a name for themselves and not to honor God. Because of that, God scattered them and confused their language. Let's look at the principle, or the truth, God says about this situation: "Behold, they are one people and they all have one language; and this is only the beginning of what they will do, and now nothing they have imagined they can do will be impossible for them." (Genesis 11:6 AMP) This is an incredible statement. Because they were *one* and *spoke the same thing* (united in heart and voice), nothing they imagined would be impossible for them. *Selah*. Even though this example was not a good thing for the kingdom of God, imagine what it could be if it were. If God finds a people who are united in heart and mind, and all speak the same thing, the possibilities to advance the kingdom are endless! He said so Himself. He's praying for the body of Christ to be one people, with one language, united in our voice. "My prayer for all of them is that they will be of one heart and mind, just as you and I are, Father—that just as you are in me and I am in you, so they will be in us, and the world will believe you sent me." (John 17:21 TLB)

While in prayer one day, I began to feel God's heart, and His heartache from being separated from His family. I felt the longing in His heart to be united once again with those He loves. He wants to be intimate with us, to spend time with us, but so often we don't have time for Him. We're too busy with our own agenda. In addition to feeling His heartache, I felt the grief in His heart over His "kids" being separated from one another. To the heart of an earthly father, it would be similar to having a son and a daughter estranged from one another, allowing circumstances to separate them to the point that they purposely do not talk. Each one thinking they know best. If that can cut the heart of an earthly father, imagine what it does to God's heart when we purposely separate ourselves from one another. God's heart is that we not only become reconciled to one another but when one of us falls, the other is there to pick them up. For too long we have judged and condemned our brothers for being weak and failing on a human level, but it is not our job to judge. It is our job to extend mercy and let God judge. He is the only one who sees all, and the only one qualified to judge with righteous judgment.

One of the greatest weapons the enemy has used against the body of Christ is a spirit of pride, which is ironic because we know that was Satan's downfall in the beginning. But pride has kept us separated, thinking we each have the correct theology. Please consider this: When God looks at us, He doesn't see denominations. Walls we have erected called "denominations" were never God's intent. His desire is that every dividing wall comes down. We don't have to agree on everything, but we do have to agree on the important points. Three main ones: Father, Son, and Holy Spirit. Let's be unified in everything the Bible says concerning our "triune leadership team" and everything else will fall into place. Any belief beyond the triune we don't necessarily have to agree on, but give grace and mercy to one another, seasoned with love.

Even in a corporate denominational people, there can be division and strife. Again, this stems from a spirit of pride, thinking we know better than our brother or sister. Remember the spirit of pride caused the downfall of the worship leader God originally had in heaven. If we are going to worship in spirit and truth corporately, the spirit of pride can have no place.

We must submit to the leadership God puts in a corporate body and trust that He knows what He's doing. Unity in a corporate body can only come as we submit to one another, and recognize and honor the gifts and callings God has put in each of us individually. As we do this, the spirit of pride will be defeated. This one thing alone will cause corporate unity and intimacy to explode.

ఆ

Prayer and Declaration: Father, forgive us that we have submitted to a spirit of pride without even realizing it. Lord, we repent for agreeing with the spirit of pride and ask forgiveness for our part in dividing the body. Lord, we declare the spirit of pride will no longer have its place in us or in the body of Christ. We break the agreement with pride right now in the name of Jesus, and declare the spirit of love and humility will reign in us. We declare the spirit of unity will be released over us and our brethren, and we will walk in the purpose and power you created us to walk in. In Jesus' mighty name we pray, amen and amen.

ఆ

A House of Love

"You shall love the Lord your God with all your heart, with all your soul, and with all your mind. This is the first and great commandment. And the second is like it. You shall love your neighbor as yourself." (Matthew 22:37-39) If God can find a corporate body that prioritizes and lives the two greatest commandments, He can release His power in an unprecedented way through that people. Let's look at one man's example, which is Christ our Lord. He came to this earth, emptied Himself of all deity, and became a man. Everything He did, He did as a man walking in complete obedience to God. He is our ultimate example of the love of God. As He washed His disciples' feet before the feast of Passover, He spoke to them "By this all will know that you are My disciples, if you have love for one another." (John 13:35) A disciple is a follower of Christ.

Loving God and others as described in the first and second commandment is not something we can work up, or stir up, within our own selves. This type of love has to be given to us by God Himself. That is why Jesus prayed to God in John 17:26, "I have declared to them your name, and will declare it, that the love with which you loved Me may be in them, and I in them." That is why we pray, "Lord, more of you and less of me." The Holy Spirit has a part in this work of love: "When the Helper [Holy Spirit)] comes, whom I shall send to you from the Father, the Spirit of truth who proceeds from the Father, He will testify of Me." (John 15:26)

There is a great mystery concerning Christ and the church that Paul talks about in Ephesians chapter five. He likens this mystery to the union of a man and woman when they marry. They forsake all others and cling to one another. This is the desire of Jesus, that His individual and corporate bride would forsake all others and cling to Him. Are we clinging to Him individually and collectively? Or do we have our own agenda? Are we too afraid of what others might think to cling to Him and to be transparent in the corporate setting? The Lord truly wants His corporate body to be a place where He can be Himself. Will we allow it? Can we be free to express ourselves to Him in a corporate setting, or is that "too much"? I don't think so.

> As soon as He was approaching [the city], at the descent of the Mount of Olives, the whole crowd of the disciples began to rejoice and to praise God [extolling Him exultantly and] loudly for all the mighty miracles and works of power that they had witnessed, crying, 'Blessed [celebrated with praises] is the King Who comes in the name of the Lord! Peace in heaven and glory [majesty, splendor] in the highest [heaven]!' Some of the Pharisees from the crowd said to Him, 'Teacher, rebuke your disciples [for shouting these Messianic praises].' Jesus replied, 'I tell you, if these [people] keep silent, the stones will cry out [in praise]!'
>
> Luke 19:37-39 AMP

This is an example of a corporate setting in which Jesus was confronted by "religious spirits" who wanted the praise silenced, but we see from His response that was not an option. Jesus wants our praise and adoration, individually and corporately. Love cannot be silenced!

A number of years ago, Pastor Jerry Howell of Destiny Christian Center spoke a prophetic word that gave us a glimpse into the future. Prophetic words are necessary for the body of Christ to continue to move forward and advance the kingdom of God. These prophetic words release revelation and are keys to moving with God into the future. "Where there is no vision [no redemptive revelation of God] the people perish ..." (Proverbs 29:18 AMP) The prophetic word Pastor Jerry released was, "Love will be the crowning glory of the end-time anointing." *Selah.* In all that God has planned for our future and future generations, love will truly be our greatest possession, our greatest anointing, and our greatest weapon. "And now abide faith, hope, love, these three; but the greatest of these is love." (1Cor 13:13) As the world grows darker, God will have a people that walk in the light and power of love. This anointing of love will produce an unprecedented glory that we have not yet seen. We are on His timetable, and the harvest is now. The glory that we are about to experience will be more than we have ever imagined.

The love God is now releasing to us individually and corporately will tear down every wall, annihilate every religious spirit, and destroy everything that would try to destroy us. His love truly will be the crowning glory. We will wear His love like a crown, and it will bring Him great glory. The end-time anointing that we are now tasting will carry His love and glory to the ends of the earth. With God, there is neither time nor space. We, as a corporate body, can stand in one spot, and release the power of love that will travel through time and space, and touch the hearts of those who need it. God's ways are magnificent. They are not held captive by boundaries. This great end-time anointing is for the harvest, and we are now 'on the cusp' of it. God will do things we've never seen because He loves the lost as much as He loves His bride. But we, as His bride, are the ones privileged to partner with Him in the great end-time harvest.

Prayer and Declaration: Father, thank you that you are filling us with the same love that you put in Jesus. That love will be so great, there will not be anything that we cannot do in the name of Jesus. Thank you, Father, for the exponential power and glory that is released in your corporate body as love is displayed. We decree, Lord, we will partner with you in whatever way you call us, realizing it may sometimes look out of the norm and break religious rules. But you, Lord, are our example. Twice, you turned over religious tables in your house. We declare every religious table will again be turned over in your house (your 'individual' houses and your corporate houses);

and in its place will be the freedom to release your love and glory. You are worthy to receive it all, Lord. In your precious name we pray, amen and amen.

៚

A Place of Refuge

Webster's dictionary defines *refuge* as "a condition of being safe or sheltered from pursuit, danger, or trouble." A refuge provides shelter. The Hebrew word for refuge is *machaceh*, which is translated as "hope". The Lord has been and always will be our place of refuge and we have many scriptures to back that up, as well as experiences. For me, His place of refuge is very real and precious, and so it should be for all of us.

God lead Ruth to a place of refuge. She chose to honor her mother-in-law, Naomi, and go back to Naomi's homeland of Judah. There, in the city of Bethlehem, the Lord led Ruth to glean in a field owned by Boaz. Boaz spoke to Ruth:

> You will listen, my daughter, will you not? Do not go to glean in another field, nor go from here, but stay close by my young women. Let your eyes be on the field which they reap, and go after them. Have I not commanded the young men not to touch you? And when you are thirsty, go to the vessels and drink from what the young men have drawn.
>
> Ruth 2:8-9

Ruth was overwhelmed that God had led her to a field that was going to be prosperous and safe. She asked Boaz why he was showing her such favor, and he responded that the kindness she had shown her mother-in-law had been reported to him. Then he said something very significant: "The Lord repay your work, and a full reward be given you by the Lord God of Israel, under whose wings you have come for refuge." (Ruth 2:12) Even though Ruth wasn't sure of what she would encounter, she chose to follow Naomi, make Naomi's home her home, and Naomi's people her people. Her mother-in-law's people were the heritage of the Lord God of Israel, and she was grafted into that heritage by her choice to follow. It was there she found a place of refuge, provision, love and redemption.

In addition to the Lord being our place of refuge, it is interesting to note that in Numbers 35:10-11, the Lord instructs Moses to appoint *cities* to be places of refuge. Have you ever considered an entire city to be a place of refuge? What about a specific place or area being a place of refuge? I believe we will experience places of refuge in the days ahead. What about your home? Is that a place of refuge for you? Even as I write this, it is a cold, dreary, rainy day outside. But here in the shelter of my home, it is warm. I have a fire blazing in the fireplace, and feel safe and secure.

Just as our homes are places of refuge, so too, God's houses (or sanctuaries) are places of refuge. He loves His family to gather in His house so He can surround us in the shelter of His wings. It is in God's house that we find an even greater dimension of safety. Sometimes when you are alone, it might be hard to get past the circumstances of life and find the place of peace. But in the corporate setting, you can find strength in your spiritual family. There are people who will surround you and make you feel safe just by their presence. There's a dimension of worship, prayer, and intercession that you can't get at home, and there is power in that atmosphere. Once you touch the Spirit of God in the corporate place, you know nothing can harm you or dissuade you from following Him completely. "He who dwells in the secret place of the Most High shall abide under the shadow of the Almighty. I will say of the Lord, 'He is my refuge and my fortress; My God, in Him I will trust.'" (Psalm 91:1-2) What a promise! David experienced that promise when God delivered him numerous times from the hand of Saul. He wrote, "The Lord is my rock and my fortress and my deliverer; the God of my strength, in whom I will trust; my shield and the horn of my salvation, my stronghold and my refuge; my Savior, you save me from violence." (2 Samuel 22:2-3)

In Hebrews 10:25, Paul instructs us not to forsake the assembling of ourselves together, and to exhort one another, especially as we see the day [of Christ's return] approaching. There is much wisdom in his words. Corporate refuge is very real and powerful. It is a place to be built up, strengthened, and encouraged. And finding the place of corporate refuge brings closeness not only to God, but also to His people. Closeness brings a oneness and unity, and as the psalmist writes:

> Behold, how good and how pleasant it is for brethren to dwell together in unity! It is like the precious oil upon the head, running down on the beard, the beard of Aaron, running down on the edge of his garments. It is like the dew of Hermon, descending upon the mountains of Zion; for there the Lord commanded the blessing—life forevermore.
>
> Psalms 133:1-3

A few years ago I had an open vision during which I experienced the reality of corporate refuge. We were in a very high and majestic place of worshipping, and I had my eyes closed. Suddenly I heard what sounded like a water dam breaking, and I opened my eyes fully expecting to see some sort of disaster, but what I saw instead was a huge, deep, clear pool, and all around me were cliffs rising as high as I could see. There was beautiful foliage climbing out of the rocky cliffs and huge waterfalls splashing down all around me. It was a very beautiful place; very peaceful in one sense with the deep blue pool, and very powerful at the same time with the waterfalls plunging down. I felt impressed in my spirit that the whole scene around me was not just a place, or a building, but it was the body of Christ, and the members made up the pool. And the pool was full of life. The water that cascaded down was directly from the throne room of heaven; it was the river of life coming down from the throne of God that is referenced in Revelation 22:1. The scripture the Lord gave me for this vision was Psalm 42:7: "[Roaring] deep calls to [roaring] deep at the thunder of your waterspouts; all your breakers and your rolling waves have gone over me." (AMP)

Have you ever had the deep of Him call unto the deep of you? It is a sound like no other. It is a place like no other, a place of refuge and power. In this place, literally, anything can happen. In a corporate place of refuge, heavens are opened and you know it is a safe place to experience all God has for you.

☙

Prayer and Declaration: Father, thank you for the provision of refuge. It is so needed in the days we live in. Lord, thank you for the places of refuge you have established for us: our homes, our corporate gatherings, and our cities. But Lord, most of all, thank you for the shelter of your wings. We decree, Lord that we will always be aware of walking under the shadow of your wings, no matter where we are. We decree, Lord, to embrace the covenant right to refuge that you have promised. And Lord, we decree there is not anything that can touch us that you are not aware of, and have not already made provision for. In Jesus' mighty name, amen and amen.

൫

A House of Power

As the vision began I was in the sanctuary, and the worship team had begun to sing and play, weaving in and out of a new sound of warfare and power, then love and intimacy. As we corporately went into a warfare mode, I saw in the vision we were a unified body; standing on a hill in what I perceived was another country, overlooking a vast valley. We couldn't see down into the valley because it was overgrown with bushes, thick brush, and broken trees. The "warfare" sound on the instruments sounded like an army marching in unity. I then saw angels descend on the valley with machetes in their hands, and they began to clear away the brush and debris with their machetes; starting at the place we stood and working their way down the valley, they were clearing paths that had been impassable.

Then the sound in the sanctuary changed to a deep love and intimate worship, mixed with intercession. I saw more angels descending with machetes to help the others cut paths down the valley. This happened over and over. As we were in the warfare mode, the angels were busy cutting paths down the valley, and when we began to sing love songs to the Lord and intercede, many more angels descended with machetes. After a while, as this happened repeatedly, I saw the angels had completely cleared the paths. Then I saw deep down into the valley, a vast multitude of weary, hurting, discouraged people huddled together. They slowly began to rise and walk up the paths that were cleared by the angels. As they walked up the paths and began to look up, a light began to shine on their faces, and new hope began to come. I sensed the Lord was releasing the light of His love and glory on them, His very essence. I watched as all the paths began to fill up with multitudes of people coming up and out, and then the vision ended.

At that moment, the worship ministry ended. As we sat in silence, the Lord dropped Song of Solomon 6:4 in my spirit. For every vision the Lord gives me, He also gives me a scripture to explain or back it up. And the word He gave this time, was for us as a corporate body. He was speaking to us, not to the multitude: "Oh my love, you are as beautiful as Tirzah, lovely as Jerusalem, awesome as an army with banners." I sensed He was very pleased with our corporate partnership with Him and the angels. In the Old Testament, the two strongest and most beautiful cities in Palestine were Tirzah and Jerusalem. And an army with banners speaks of a victorious army coming back from battle. Hallelujah!

What happened during our corporate worship released angels, and we partnered with them to accomplish His purpose. I have no doubt that somewhere in the earth that vision was literally being "played out," and there truly were people being released to come up and out of captivity. There is such power in corporate unity.

In the corporate setting, there is also a multiplicity that comes from unity. Exponential power and anointing are released. The power in unity can be so strong that God will begin to move in a congregation to heal, deliver, and set people free, without anyone praying or laying hands on them. I have also experienced people sharing their testimony of God healing them, and as they do, faith is released, and the same miracle of healing happens to one or more people in the congregation. You might ask, "What has this got to do with corporate intimacy?" When everyone's eyes are on Him there is a unified intimacy in the corporate setting. It creates a synergy and an atmosphere for Him to work. When we allow the Holy Spirit to reign in our midst, He can reveal Jesus in a way like no other. There are countless numbers of examples in scripture of Jesus revealing His power corporately. We will experience this in a much greater measure as time goes on. His Word says, "Of the increase of His government and peace there will be no end ..." (Isaiah 9:7) That means MORE!

There is one last example I will share that demonstrates the power of corporate unity. I was in a worship service at my home church in 1999, and the musicians were leading the congregation in a high song of praise right out of the book of Revelation 7. We were singing in unity a song, "All power, all honor, all glory to you, O God." In that atmosphere of agreement with who God is, I experienced an open vision. As I looked up, the first heaven literally rolled back like a scroll, and I saw into the second heaven; the place where principalities and powers of Satan's realm dwell. Looking into that second heaven, and still while worshipping and agreeing with God's very nature as we sang, I saw satanic music in our area being displaced. The word *displaced* was the word I actually heard in my spirit, and perceived by the Spirit of God to be happening. The word *displace* means "(1) to compel to leave one's home, country, etc. (2) to move or put out of the usual or proper place (3) to supplant (4) to remove from a position or office, and finally (5) to make obsolete; to rid oneself of." That, my beloved, is the power of unity in worship! We were simply coming into agreement with who God says He is. That vision caused me to understand another way to war. We never once addressed principalities or powers of satanic music, but only came in agreement in worship with who God is. Then God demonstrated what we were declaring. Beloved, this type of worship and unity is what God can use to change regions. It will require us laying down preconceived ideas and agendas and coming into agreement with His. Do you want it badly enough? God is looking for those who desperately want it and will pay the price for unity in every area.

So let's delve again into the question posed at the beginning of this chapter: Is corporate intimacy fact or fiction?

160

From all scripture quotes, examples of corporate visions, healings, and love released, I would have to say an emphatic yes! God is all about corporate intimacy. He absolutely loves it. Corporate intimacy releases love and unity. It creates a refuge. It displays power. Your one-on-one time with God in the secret place encompasses the first commandment, and corporate intimacy encompasses the second.

⊙✢⊚

Prayer and Declaration: Father, thank you for revealing the power available to us corporately. Thank you that you will partner with us to fulfill your purpose and plan. Forgive us, Lord, for thinking the corporate place is all about us, when it's all about you. It is about your power, your love, and your agenda. Show us, Lord, how to move as one with you and experience the excitement of watching your plan unfold. We decree, Lord, that corporate intimacy will become a part of us. Lord, we declare we will be a people who will fulfill the call to love you with all of our hearts, all our minds, all our soul and all our strength. We will be a people who love others as ourselves. You need not look for anyone else. We will be your people, Lord. We declare it is you who causes us both to will and to do your good pleasure. And it is you who will fulfill all that is in your heart through us. In Jesus' mighty name, amen and amen.

⊙✢⊚

Reflections on Chapter Five

1. List three ways your corporate worship is a response to God directly. Be very specific.

2. God desires denominational walls to come down. How are you promoting the unity God desires in His entire corporate body and bride?

3. How does your corporate worship express the love of God? Be specific. Name one thing you can begin to do to more fully express your love for God in the corporate setting.

CHAPTER 6

Last But Not Least …
The Resting Place

In the secret place with God, there comes a time when we go past our prayers, petitions, and any form of activity. We enter a place of rest. In the spiritual realm, it is His rest. Entering into rest releases His power to work in situations. Rest is much better than striving. It is actually a higher place of authority because as we rest in Him, everything becomes about Him. We take His hand to come into agreement, we know His heart because we've spent time with Him, and now we rest and listen. What comes next is the revelation of His plan and purpose. We begin to decree and release what is in His heart. These decrees are giving voice to what He is revealing. This is partnering with Him to bring His kingdom to the earth. No striving, but complete trust.

While on a mission trip in the fall of 1992, Pastor Jerry Howell of Destiny Christian Center had a powerful word from God. As Pastor Jerry was traveling by train in Germany, God spoke a *rhema* word to him out of Isaiah 66:1 "Where is the house you will build me? And where is the place of my rest?" These two questions resonated in Pastor Jerry's heart as he pondered what they meant. The Lord then spoke over his right shoulder and into his ear, "I'm striving in my own house." This statement, along with the word from Isaiah 66:1, became a life word and work to Pastor Jerry, as he set out to create the house God asked for. God wanted a house that He wouldn't have to compete or rival anything or anyone but completely rest. *Strive* means "to contend in opposition, battle or conflict; to compete; to rival." God's desire is that when and wherever His people gather, He will be able to rest and create in our midst.

When God created woman, He caused Adam to rest, and He created out of that rest. "And the Lord God caused a deep sleep to fall on Adam, and he slept; and He took one of his ribs, and closed up the flesh in its place. Then the rib which the Lord God had taken from man He made into a woman, and he brought her to the man." (Genesis 2: 21-22) There is a valuable lesson for us to glean from this. Remember resting, especially in warfare, is a higher place of authority because it becomes all about Him. We are vessels for Him to flow His desires through. We hear, and then we declare and decree. We hear, and we release the word that creates. We are a conduit of His living word. We release, and He backs up His word with action.

In Genesis 8 we read the story of Noah and the flood. When the flood waters receded enough for the ark to rest on top of Ararat, Noah sent a dove out of the ark. Twice the dove came back, but the third time the dove found a place of rest and did not return to the ark. Noah then knew the time of transition had come. Like the dove, this is what God wants, not only in His people but in His house. He wants a place where He can rest and just BE. In an atmosphere of rest, our hearts are comforted, our minds quieted, and we are able to hear and see more clearly. The time for this transition of rest is upon us.

God doesn't want us to go in and out of His rest; He is about abiding. That is His desire. His heart longs for us to abide in Him as He abides in us. He wants us to live and occupy in the rest. That is so different from the world's standard. The world tells us we need to push, shove, make things happen, get more, take more, and do more. There is a much better way: It is living and occupying in the rest. What does living in the rest look like? How does it sound? How does it feel? Living and occupying in the rest produces an experience that empowers you: "...in returning and rest you shall be saved; in quietness and confidence shall be your strength..." (Isaiah 30:15)

❧

Prayer and Declaration: Father, forgive us for the times we have been so busy trying to make things happen on our own when you have provided all we need as we rest in you. We repent for not trusting you enough to let you lead. Father, we decree as we turn to you, we will enter the rest you have ordained, and we will find our answers in that rest. Thank you, Lord that your provision is perfect and complete. In Jesus' name, amen and amen.

❧

Warfare from a Place of Rest

In 2004, the Lord gave me a strategic vision concerning spiritual warfare. This vision has been instrumental in my walk with Him and has taught me much about warfare. This particular vision has also been the only time I have had a two-phase vision. Let me explain. I had been repenting of wrong attitudes and anger towards a couple of people I love dearly but felt they had made some bad choices out of selfishness. I was driving home from work when suddenly I was "transported" to the throne room in heaven. I knew I was there to do spiritual warfare. From this higher place, my anger towards those I love had been re-directed towards the enemy. The Lord held out a scepter to me, I touched it, and then heard Him say "Go for it!" I turned and looked down, fully realizing I was in the third heaven, above the principalities and powers. I knew the Lord was giving me the authority to war against them from that position. I began to bind the enemy, speak to the demons that were involved in this assignment of destruction against those I loved, and declare victory over the situation. I realized I already had the victory; I just had to speak it out! It was an incredible time of spiritual warfare.

Later that night, I went upstairs to my prayer room and spent a little time waiting on the Lord. I felt the warfare "mode" still kind of stirring in my spirit, but after about twenty minutes, nothing came forth, so I started back downstairs. It was then that I heard the Holy Spirit say, "I'm not finished yet!" I turned around and went back into my room, and as soon as I shut the door behind me, I was immediately back in the throne room. I heard God say, "There is a better way." I knew He was referring to spiritual warfare. I turned toward Him, took His hand that was extended to mine, and closed my eyes. I began to "hear" in my spirit His desire for the two people I had been in spiritual warfare over earlier in the day. As I held His hand with mine, I had the other stretched down towards the earth, and I actually felt like I was touching each person. I felt like a "human conduit". As God was speaking into my spirit His desires for each person, they were flowing through me and going into the person. He reminded me again of the first *rhema* word He had ever given me "You have not chosen me, I have chosen you, and ordained you, that you might go and bear fruit, and your fruit will remain, so that whatever you ask the Father in my name, He may give it to you." (John 15:16) So, as His desires for each one flowed through me and down to them, I saw "fruit" begin to spring forth from each life.

Later, as I pondered this powerful vision, I understood the full impact of what God was saying. The first place of spiritual warfare I had been in earlier in the day actually sprang forth from emotions of anger and injustice. Although it was legitimate, that warfare was really about me and my feelings. In contrast, the second place of warfare was a state of rest and peace, flowing with God's plan of justice. The rest and peace were a better way, even though I felt complete confidence in the Lord in both types of warfare.

In this two-part vision, God allowed me to experience a higher form of warfare by contrasting the earlier vision with the latter one. Both were effective and legitimate, but the latter was more powerful for a couple of reasons. One, it was truly God's heart of justice and was not based on my emotions. As Gary Wiens states in His book *Bridal Intercession*, "God's justice is the full restoration of all things according to the original design held in His mind from the foundation of the world." Secondly, this warfare from a place of rest produced fruit that proved to be everlasting. This is true bridal intercession and is a key that will unlock the secrets of His heart and produce lasting results in our prayers. This type of prayer and declarations are what the

Holy Spirit is revealing to the bride of Christ during these end times. It is one of the ways we are privileged to partner with Him. *Selah.*

Covenant Rest

"There remains therefore a rest for the people of God. For he who has entered His rest has himself also ceased from his works as God did from His." (Hebrews 4:9-10) God created the world in six days and then rested from His work on the seventh day, the day of completion. He expects us to rest from our works as well. When we come to a place in our spiritual growth when we know who He really is and who we are in Him, we enter a higher level of understanding. That higher place is the doorway into His covenant rest. We can rest because we understand we are in covenant with the One who is the creator of all.

Hebrews goes on to say, "Let us therefore be diligent to enter that rest, lest anyone fall according to the same example of disobedience." (Hebrews 4:11) The writer of Hebrews is referring to God's people who came out of Egypt, led by Moses. They did not enter the Promised Land, the place of rest, because of unbelief and hardened hearts. The writer calls this an example of disobedience. Have you ever considered unbelief to be disobedience? *Selah.* This should give us cause to examine our own lives. Are there places in your heart where you have a hard time believing God's word?

Maybe it is in the area of healing, or speaking in tongues. Or it could be the belief that God won't do miracles for you because you are not worthy. Let's examine our hearts and be sure we are not walking in disobedience. Our hearts can cause us to fail to enter the covenant rest that God has intended for us as the body and bride of Christ. The word says to be diligent to enter into that rest. This is where our warfare lies: In being diligent to enter into His covenant rest. Be determined to have no unbelief or hardness of heart in any area. In spite of our struggles, God will never break His covenant with us. His covenant is a sure foundation now and forever. It will never die, grow old, or fade away. His covenant is as strong now as the day He hung on the cross and died for us.

In the place of covenant rest God will show us things we wouldn't otherwise be able to see. He wants to partner with us in covenant, to bring justice to the earth. As He does the work, we can rest in the knowledge that His ways are perfect and complete. He revealed this to me, once again, in a strategic dream. I was on the side of a mountain, and the Lord came and "flew" me to the top. He was in bodily form, not the form of an eagle; and then we began leaping together from one mountain top to another. We stopped on one of the mountains and He looked down into the valley, then turned to me and said, "What do you see?" I looked down into the valley far below us, and I could see with "eagle" eyes. I not only saw with great clarity, but with complete understanding. I saw human trafficking and young girls in chains, being abused. He then said to me, "What should we do about it?" As I was pondering how to answer, I suddenly felt overwhelmed with Father God's heart. I was actually feeling His heart and understood with great clarity exactly how He saw it, and the injustice He was feeling. I began to declare "Freedom!" to the young girls and declared chains were being broken to set captives free. There was a mass exodus as the chains fell off the girls and they began to run, full of joy and freedom from captivity. The Lord smiled and then took my hand, and off we went to another mountain top. Then I woke up.

In a place of covenant rest, we as the bride of Christ will move in the authority and power of our Lord. He wants us to fly high with Him like eagles on the various mountains of society, warring against injustice according to His purpose and plan. "For in Him we live and move and have or being" (Acts 17:28) Again, warring in and through Him, from a place of rest, is a higher place of understanding and authority. "... to whom much is given, from him much will be required." (Luke 12:48) This authority is not available to the casual seeker or the faint of heart, but to those who have their senses trained, discerning evil and good. This is the privilege of the bride of Christ, moving in the authority of who He is.

Being an intercessor for many years, and warring and pushing through in prayer so many times, I sometimes forget that God has told me there is a better way. He reminded me of that recently and demonstrated that He meant what He said, in reference to warring from a place of covenant rest.

It was October 31, 2015: I woke up feeling a strong sense of evil. Then, in the spirit, I saw three teenage girls sitting around a campfire with voodoo dolls and bowls of some type of liquid. There was a spirit of witchcraft being released into the atmosphere, through incantations, curses, and spells. I knew the Holy Spirit was allowing me to see this in the spirit to warfare over. Of course, on Halloween, too, there is always increased demonic activity. I got out of bed to go pray and war over what I saw. As I started down the hallway, I began to speak out and plead the blood of Jesus. Suddenly, I saw the heavens open and angels came down with huge chains. They slung the chains around the ones involved in the witchcraft and rendered them helpless. Then I felt the evil lift and depart. It was over! I thought I was really going to have to war over this thing with "blood, sweat, and tears," but, by revelation and pleading the blood, God overcame in a matter of seconds. Incredible! This was a perfect example of warring from a place of rest that came from and out of covenant.

❧

Prayer and Declaration: Father, thank you for your covenant with us. Thank you, Lord, that we can rest in that covenant,

174

*knowing you are the one who never breaks a covenant.
Lord, teach us how to fully rest in your covenant; how to
live and move and have our being in you alone. Your ways
are so much higher than ours, Lord, and your thoughts so
much higher. Father, we decree we will learn how to rest and
allow your covenant to fully manifest in us. We declare Lord,
that covenant rest will become "second nature" to us, and
our trust in you will grow through it. Thank you for the gift
of covenant rest. In Jesus' name, I pray, amen and amen.*

ॐ

Creative Rest

There is creativity that comes from rest, as we see in the
following scripture in Genesis. God could have created
woman any way He wanted, but He chose to create her in
rest. We can learn a lot from this example. Since God chooses
to create from rest, why not us?

> And the Lord God caused a deep sleep [rest] to fall
> on Adam, and he slept; and He took one of his ribs,
> and closed up the flesh in its place. Then the rib
> which the Lord God had taken from man He made
> into woman, and He brought her to the man. And
> Adam said, 'This is now bone of my bones and flesh
> of my flesh; She shall be called Woman, because she
> was taken out of Man.'
>
> Genesis 2:21-23

Another example of creative rest is found in John 6 when Jesus fed the five thousand. Jesus told His disciples, "Make the people sit down." As the disciples distributed the few loaves and fishes they had, the Lord miraculously multiplied the food to feed the five thousand, with twelve baskets left over. The people were hungry, and as they followed Jesus' instruction to sit down and rest, the Lord provided what they needed. This is an example of trusting to the point that we know, sometimes in our need, there is nothing we can do but wait and rest. We know that we alone cannot make anything happen. This is a form of trusting.

God is infinitely creative, and there are times He shows me His creativity in ways that boggle my mind. We sometimes have preconceived ideas about how something should look, or how to do something just because we've always done it that way. But God is not limited by time, space or any other thing. The further along we go in these end times, God will delight and surprise us with His creativity, and He will give us His wisdom in ways we never dreamed possible.

I had a dream a couple of years ago that caused me to understand the importance of resting so God can create. This is the only dream I have ever had that started out in black and white and ended in glorious color. In my dream, a lady came into the store where I was and began to buy things "stuck away" that nobody else wanted. She was buying everything that we thought was of no value. She also bought bolts and bolts of cloth and asked me to re-wrap them. I tried to re-wrap them and she said, "No, that's not the way! Do it over." I wrapped and rewrapped, but could never get it right to her liking, so in frustration, I tossed it behind me and went into the next room to sit down and rest. I had only been sitting a short time when I heard a loud trumpet blast behind me (at this point my black and white dream turned into living Technicolor). I turned and saw a glorious army coming forth, clothed in the fabric I had tossed aside. But the fabric didn't look at all like it had before. It was now shimmering and seemed to exude life. This army was magnificent, marching in perfect rank, and clothed in the glory of God; so powerful and awesome, I fell backwards at their splendor. I ran and got a priest, and we both stood in awe at the sight of them. Then the dream ended.

I pondered this dream for some time, and then the Lord gave the interpretation. The lady was the church, receiving the people nobody wanted. The cloth was the wineskin that had grown old, but we were still trying to fit it into the mold and the image we thought it should have been. But now, the Lord is changing the wineskin, and it is not by our power or strength, but by His Spirit. The people nobody wanted are now coming forth in glorious splendor, like a mighty army, clothed in Him. We have heard many opinions and ideas about what the new wineskin is, but I believe the new wineskin is Him alone. His glory and His splendor; it is all about Him! We will be fully clothed in Him. "… but they put new wine into new wineskins, and both are preserved." (Matthew 9:17) So let me ask you, what wineskin are you counting on to preserve you?

Then the Lord gave me the scripture to confirm what I was hearing:

> … and to make all see what is the fellowship of the mystery which from the beginning of the ages has been hidden in God who created all things through Jesus Christ; to the intent that now the manifold wisdom of God might be made known by the church to the principalities and powers in the heavenly places, according to the eternal purpose which He accomplished in Christ Jesus our Lord, in whom we have boldness and access with confidence through faith in Him.
>
> Ephesians 3:9-12

Selah! God has a plan concerning His corporate bride, and it is causing the enemy to tremble as he sees the plan coming to pass. It cannot be stopped.

❧

Prayer and Declaration: Thank you, Lord, for your creative rest. Lord, forgive us for the times we think we have to make things happen on our own, and we don't allow you the opportunity to reveal who you really are and what you can do. Forgive us, Lord, for not accessing the mind of Christ the way we need to. Lord, we declare we will begin now to ask and access by faith the fathomless mind of Christ, in all of your creativity and wisdom. Lord, we decree access to things we have not yet seen or imagined. We decree a release of your creativity into our minds and hearts and declare that creativity will catapult us into a new realm of understanding and authority. In Jesus' mighty name, amen and amen.

☙

Reflections on Chapter Six

1. Have you discovered the secret of resting in the Lord for everything you need on a daily basis? If not, what is hindering your rest, or trust; and how can you change it?

2. How does your spiritual warfare look from a place of rest? How does it feel? Name one thing you can do to make it more effective.

3. Can you see the correlation between God's covenant and His rest? In what areas of your life are you having a hard time entering into God's covenant rest?

_____

_____

_____

_____

_____

_____

_____

_____

_____

CHAPTER 7

The Challenge Ahead

There are several challenges we face to come into a place of intimacy with God; but with each of these challenges, God has the ability to bring us into victory. I will address several of the challenges in this chapter, but remember one very important thing: God's desire is for us to be completely His, and He will work with us in each of these areas, as we yield to Him. "For it is God who works in you both to will and to do for His good pleasure." (Philippians 2:13) He loves us so, and His heart is for us to move and live and have our being in Him. No time outs, no breaks, no moving in and out of our abiding place in Him; one with Him at all times, and in all places. So the good news is, no matter what we might be lacking in, He has us covered. Yes, we will experience some growing pains, and it won't be pleasant at the time,

183

but it is part of the process of becoming the mature bride of Christ, without spot or wrinkle. And that, my friend, is worth it all.

Seeing with Eyes of Understanding

First, we must agree with Him about who we are: the good, the bad and the ugly. We cannot hide anything from Him. Of course, He knows everything about us anyway. But when we vocalize our issues, a spiritual transfer takes place that we cannot see in the natural realm. Remember, the invisible spiritual world is so much more real than the physical world in which we see and hear and touch things.

For example, if the Holy Spirit reveals to you a spirit of pride in your life, the best way to deal with it is to acknowledge it, ask forgiveness, repent of the pride, and ask the Lord to help you. Then begin to decree the spirit of pride is broken and is being replaced by a spirit of humility in your life. This is a powerful declaration and action in the spirit. First of all, it takes away the power of the enemy over the pride in your life. Secondly, it allows the Lord to begin to work on you in that area, to bring you into humility.

We all have things in our life that we must deal with. But to get real with God is a powerful action that produces lasting fruit in your life. This is a key to being able to come into intimacy with God.

Release Your Fears

Easier said than done? No one knows that feeling better than I. Let me give you just one example of many I have experienced. Several years ago, I had been through one of the hardest seasons I can remember in a long time. Feeling overwhelmed, pressured, fearful, discouraged, and beat down, I asked the Lord to change my boundaries; to not let anyone set the course of my life except Him. As I prayed and pressed into Him for this, He gave me a vision of, once again, being at the banqueting table with Him.

He was across from me, but talking and visiting with others sitting at the table. I felt all around me the enemies of my soul, standing on either side of me, behind me, and even behind Jesus who was across from me. My enemies were all staring at me with hatred. Fear was first in the circle, then doubt, standing shoulder to shoulder. Unbelief was next, and standing close in line was discouragement, shame, and guilt. I was virtually surrounded. I fixed my gaze on Jesus and kept it there until He looked my way, concerned. I said, "Come and fight for me! Jesus, I need you to fight for me!" I saw a holy fire in His eyes as He slammed the palms of His hands down on the table, and stood up abruptly. Immediately, all of my enemies fell backward. At that exact moment the vision ended, and I felt a release in my spirit and soul. I was free! He gave me a scripture for that encounter: "You prepare a table before me in the presence of my enemies..." (Psalm 23:5)

This was a powerful vision and taught me a couple of very key things. One, when God gets ready to release you from something, there is no demon in hell that can stop it. He can release you from a myriad of negative forces in your life as you yield to Him. I pondered this vision for quite some time and came to a second conclusion: "There is no fear in love; but perfect love casts out fear, because fear involves torment. But he who fears has not been made perfect in love." (1 John 4:18) I understood the perfect love of Jesus was tangibly released through that vision and dispelled every fear and torment I had. He does not give us His perfect love based on our being good enough. It is based on His mercy, grace, and goodness.

I'll tell you a precious truth the enemy would like us to never see or understand: If you are His, perfect love is a covenant gift. All you have to do is receive it. "You see, you have not received a spirit that returns you to slavery, so you have nothing to fear. The Spirit you have received adopts you and welcomes you into God's own family. That's why we call out to Him 'Abba! Father!' as we would address a loving daddy." (Romans 8:15 The Voice) "If we are God's children, that means we are His heirs along with the Anointed, set to inherit everything that is His…" (Romans 8:17 The Voice)

Facing the Trust Issue

"For I know the plans I have for you," declares the Lord, "plans to prosper you and not to harm you, plans to give you hope and a future." (Jeremiah 29:11 NIV) The question is do you believe this? If not, then it is time to get to know God a little better. He has good plans for you. His plans will give you hope and excitement about your future. He sent His Son to die for you, that His plan might be fulfilled. He's paid for everything you need to secure your future. He's given you His promises.

It is time to stop believing the lie of the enemy that there is anything bigger than God, that there's something more powerful than Him that can thwart His plans. There is not. Ask God to help you with unbelief, and to heal those things in the past that keep you from trusting Him completely. Release your fears to Him. You might say, "How can I do that? I've been hurt and disappointed too many times, and I don't want to be hurt again." To that person, I would suggest you give it just one more try. Only, take a chance with the One who will not disappoint. Try it just once more with the one who treasures your heart and holds it gently. You'll find He is a safe Savior. He's a safe Father. The more you know Him, the more you will be able to let go of your past. When you put your past in His hands, He can release you into your future.

Webster's dictionary defines *trust* as "(1) reliance on the integrity, strength, ability, surety, etc. of a person or thing; confidence. (2) Confident expectation of something; hope." God's plans are to give you hope and a future. There is only one prerequisite: Know (yada) Him. Intimately know Him, and as you do, trusting and believing will come easily.

Another way to demonstrate your trust in Him is to spend time in His presence before rushing out into your day. This action of waiting demonstrates trust and is much more effectual than rushing out to complete your to-do list. This type of trust weakens principalities and powers of darkness in the spirit realm. As our trust is manifested in the spirit realm, this causes the enemy to tremble. There is power in intimate waiting and trusting.

Contend for the Faith

To fight for what we believe in is sometimes very necessary in our journey into intimacy with God. "Beloved … .I found it necessary to write to you exhorting you to contend earnestly for the faith which was once for all delivered to the saints." (Jude 1:3) In this passage, Jude was exhorting the Christians of that day to press into the foundational faith they received from the apostles who originally taught them. I believe what He wrote, inspired by the Holy Spirit, can pertain to any part of our faith, including faith to step into intimacy. Jude admonishes us to contend earnestly for our faith. Are you willing to contend for the faith in intimacy? We contend for correct doctrine, demonstrations of apostolic power, and living holy lifestyles … but will we contend for intimacy?

Beloved, Jesus had us on his mind when He entered into Jerusalem that last week of His life on earth. That truly was the week of His passion. But remember, everything He did, He did as a man. He was in violent warfare to complete the plan to win His bride back. He was contending for the right to intimacy with His bride. We were on His mind in the Garden of Gethsemane when He sweat great drops of blood to fulfill His purpose and win us back. "Looking unto Jesus, the author and finisher of our faith, who for the joy that was set before Him endured the cross, despising the shame, and has sat down at the right hand of the throne of God." (Hebrews 12:2) We were His joy, the prize set before Him. When Jesus hung on the cross and died, that was a culmination of the warfare He endured to bring forth the Father's plan to redeem His bride. And the final act of that plan, His resurrection and ascension, defied all logic, all natural reasoning, and every demon in hell. The plan was a success!

He is our example. Like Him, we must sometimes enter into that "violent warfare" in order to enter into intimacy with Him. Warfare is necessary when distractions and duties pull us in all directions, and we must strive to enter a place of rest in Him. Even as I write this, I have struggled this morning with this very thing. I have felt the frustration due to deadlines and other commitments pulling me in all directions. Only when I sat down to write, did I feel the peace and manifest presence of God envelope me in a very real way. So I know I am on the right path He ordained for me this morning. "… the kingdom of heaven suffers violence, and the violent take it by force." (Matthew 11:12) We will sometimes have to contend with the enemy to enter into God's rest; we will also have to contend with the enemy, through declarations and decrees in prayer, to advance the kingdom of God.

Another example of 'violent warfare' is found in Song of Solomon:

> By night on my bed I sought the one I love; I sought Him, but I did not find Him. 'I will rise now, I said, and go about the city; in the streets and in the squares I will seek the One I love.' I sought Him but I did not find Him. The watchmen who go about the city found me; I said 'Have you seen the One I love?' Scarcely had I passed by them [the watchmen] when I found the one I love. I held Him and would not let Him go…
>
> Song of Solomon 3:1-4

In this passage, the bride is looking for her beloved. She has always been able to find Him easily, but now she has to rise up out of her comfortable place because He has hidden Himself from her. It is a test — does she love Him enough to go search for Him? Does she love Him enough to get out of her comfort zone? She asks the watchmen if they have seen Him, but they haven't. They are focused on their assignment. But the bride has a place beyond assignment; her place is an intimate relationship. So she goes a little farther … and she finds Him. Herein lies a secret that some miss: Contending for intimacy will many times demand going a little farther; past the normal routine, past your comfort zone and familiar places, and beyond the assignments and ministries. Deep relationship sometimes demands more, but there is a great reward that comes with it. Be willing to contend for what's important to you. Be willing to fight for what you love. "And you will seek Me and find Me, when you search for Me with all your heart." (Jeremiah 29:13)

First Things First

Jesus said, "You shall love the Lord your God with all your heart, with all your soul, and with all your mind. This is the first and greatest commandment." (Matthew 22:37-38) This is undoubtedly our greatest pursuit. Even though it is a lifelong quest that we will still be working on when our time has come to stand before Him in heaven, consider our example of Jesus. He fulfilled this commandment every day of His life here on earth as a man, empowered by the Holy Spirit. He was the embodiment of the first commandment. He proved it was possible. While we are not Him, we can learn from His example.

Jesus went on to say, "And the second [commandment] is like it; You shall love your neighbor as yourself." If we try to live out the second commandment without the first in its proper place, we will experience burnout. Relationships don't work very well when you seek to love another wholeheartedly without first loving God. That's why Jesus could look at every person with love; because He was seeing them through eyes of love. He was seeing them not necessarily as they were, standing before Him, but He saw them in the original design God intended for them, which was perfect and unique. He saw past the imperfections into the person that was whole and without sin. We can only see that way as we love God with all of our heart, soul, and spirit and allow Him to remake us.

If you are a single person reading this right now and desire to have a God-ordained mate, then the first commandment becomes more important than ever. Because God knows the mate He has for you, He has a strategic plan for bringing you both together. When you pursue the first commandment in your own life, in all probability, the one in your future is also pursuing God with his or her whole heart (would you have it any other way?). When God's appointed time comes, there is a divine meeting of body, soul, and spirit. This is when love in the human arena will literally explode and erupt with love, passion, and devotion. God's plan is to bring you someone who is like-minded, and join you together for His purpose and plan.

If you are currently married, pursuing the first commandment will only strengthen your commitment. Seeing your spouse through the eyes of God's love will be the solution to the myriad challenges that couples face. As we put the first commandment into action, we learn to err on the side of mercy instead of judgement. When we look through the eyes and feel with the heart of Jesus, we will be able to judge every situation and circumstance rightly, and know what to say and do in any situation. This can be applied not only in our marriages but in every relationship we have.

Understand the Time

The church is in a time of awakening and reformation like never before in history. Right now everything around us is changing quickly, and to move forward through this lifestyle shift, our number one priority must be to stay close to God. Intimacy with the Lord is foundational and is the platform that everything else should be built upon. It is out of love and intimacy that He will reveal the secrets of His heart, the battle plans, and the strategies to take our cities and nations for Him.

The transformation we are now in will cause us to see and experience the kingdom of God as He intended. We are on God's timetable for revelation and experience. Will we choose to move with Him, or be left behind? There is a charge to us as His bride to work with Him to advance the kingdom. But intimacy and time with Him must come first!

In the worship that is now being released into the earth, there are many different kinds of songs and sounds coming forth; there are new warfare songs and sounds, as well as spontaneous love songs from His psalmists that are a part of this new sound. These songs have been stored up until the time of fullness, which is now. God is calling forth His bride with the sound of these songs, because now is the time for His love in us to be awakened. Ask for ears to hear and perceive the new sound. Ask for your heart to vibrate in tune with the new sound. Ask for wisdom and understanding to be able to prophecy and decree what the sound is saying in the spiritual realm, and then use your voice to release it in the natural realm.

God will sometimes give visions or dreams to cause us to understand the times and seasons we are in. A number of years ago, I was taken up into an open trance that caused me to understand what God was doing in the earth at that time. Sometimes He will choose unusual and miraculous means to reveal important insights to us, or to impart significant revelation or anointing. Many times, God will release revelation so we can pray and intercede for a continuation or a greater release of what we are being shown.

As I was driving home from work one afternoon, I suddenly became very aware of my hands on the steering wheel. I glanced down at them and then back up. Suddenly, I was transported into the throne room of heaven. I was aware of someone standing right beside me, possibly the angel who brought me there. In awe, I looked and saw a magnificent throne with intensely bright light around it. I saw someone sitting on the throne wearing a long robe. Although I knew in my heart it was Father God, I could not see His face. In front of Him and before the throne was a lampstand with seven flames of fire. "…Seven lamps of fire were burning before the throne, which are the seven spirits of God." (Revelation 4:5). I knew I was seeing the seven-fold Holy Spirit talked about in Isaiah 11:2, "The Spirit of the Lord shall rest upon Him, the Spirit of wisdom and understanding, the Spirit of counsel and might, the Spirit of knowledge and of the fear of the Lord." I took one step forward, and when I did, Father God leaned forward and blew on the seven flames. I felt like I was experiencing this in slow motion as the flames went into my chest like static electricity. They felt like they were pulsating and awakening every nerve in my body. Then, as quickly as I had come, I was back in my car. It seemed like all that happened in just a matter of seconds.

This open vision was not just for me, but God pulled back the veil and released a revelation of what He was doing at that time. "… the seven spirits of God sent out into all the earth." (Revelation 5:6) And the vision is for whosoever will receive it.

Count the Cost

We have looked at several challenges to moving into a deeper place with God. So the final question is … are you willing to pay the price? Sometimes the stakes are high. In April of 2004, the Lord woke me three different times in the night and said, "Count the cost." At that time in my life, I was struggling with a choice I had to make, and I knew it wasn't going to be easy. I loved the Lord so much, but was being drawn into things the world had to offer. Those things were very desirable to me, but yet I knew if I chose them, I would not be putting God first in my life. It took me awhile, but I did make the choice. I counted the cost. "…if you want to be My disciple, it will cost you everything. Don't underestimate that cost!" (Luke 14:33 The Voice) What is the cost? What will it cost *you* to be His true and faithful bride, arrayed in glorious splendor, without spot or wrinkle, holy and faultless? "Christ's love makes the church whole. His words evoke her beauty. Everything He does and says is designed to bring the best out of her, dressing her in dazzling white silk radiant with holiness." (Ephesians 5:26-27 MSG) Beloved, His way, though it costs you greatly at times, is worth every bit of momentary pain you have to endure to say no to your flesh. It is worth it. He's worth it.

As the bride of Christ, it's time to raise our standard of discipline and dedication to a higher level. Once you've counted the cost and know you're willing to give it all for Him, there is nothing that can stop your forward movement in Him. This is where victory in every area is assured. "And they overcame him [the accuser, the enemy] by the blood of the Lamb and by the word of their testimony, and they did not love their lives to the death." (Revelation 12:11) This is the place of total victory. This is the authority intended for the bride from the foundations of the world. And it all begins with an invitation into His chambers.

☙❧

Prayer and Declaration: Lord, I see the challenges that lie ahead in order to experience true intimacy with you. But Lord, I know you will help me to overcome every obstacle. You said, Lord, that you will defeat every enemy that tries to steal my heart from you. I just say, "Yes, Lord." Every obstacle is an enemy to us becoming as one. Father, I speak to those obstacles now and say they will not have dominion in my life. The challenges will not prevail over me. Lord, I declare I will advance to the place where I live and move and have my being in you. I understand, Lord, that it all comes out of the place of intimacy. So I declare, Lord, that knowing you will be my first priority, and everything else will follow. In Jesus' name, I pray, amen and amen.

☙❧

Reflections of Chapter Seven

1. What areas of unbelief and trust are holding you back from intimacy with God? Write them down. Ask Him to reveal and heal those areas in your life.

_____

_____

_____

_____

_____

_____

_____

2. Name three ways you can contend for intimacy with God. These will be NEW ways that you have not contended before.

_____

_____

_____

_____

_____

_____

_____

_____

3. Have you counted the cost of a deeper commitment to intimacy with God? What does that cost look like for you? How will you move forward in that commitment?

Epilogue

In the pages of this book, I have talked about a form of communication that is superior to what we've had in the past. You might say, how can our communication with God be better than it is right now? He's taught us how and what to pray. He's given us the Holy Spirit. He's released His seven-fold spirit. He's given us His word: *logos, rhema* and *zoe.* He's given us the gift of tongues, the heavenly bridal language. What mode of communication could be superior to all of this? God's kingdom is ever increasing, and that says to me there is always more.

I believe we are headed into an even higher channel of communication that will come through intimacy with God. *It will come from being so connected to His heart that we are an extension of Him in the deepest sense possible.* We want to take every form of prayer, every spiritual gift available to us, every tool, and every mode of communication He's given us, and use them all. The key here is not just to use them, but filter them through, and out of, an intimate relationship with Him. This is communication in its highest form. This was the communication between Father, Son, and the Holy Spirit. I don't pretend to know everything about this, but I know there have been times, brief moments, that He has allowed me to experience being an extension of His heart. To have God share His heart is a very precious thing, and not to be taken lightly. He says, "...to whom much is given, from him much will be required." (Luke 12:48)

God wants to reveal the secrets of His heart. He wants to be known by His lover just as we do. He wants someone who will pay the price to know Him intimately. There is an authority, when intimacy is unlocked, that is not to be found anywhere else. Intimate authority equals intimate adventure. Our adventuresome God wants to plan and order the steps of our day, and I can testify that life in Him, walking with the Holy Spirit, is the most exciting adventure of all. This adventure causes me to wake each day with expectation of the divine appointments God has waiting on my path. "For the law of the Spirit of Life in Jesus Christ has made me free from the law of sin and death." (Romans 8:2) Are you ready to be invaded and energized with the Spirit of Life? Are you ready to experience the power of intimacy with God? Accept the invitation into His chambers. Just say, *"Yes, Lord!"*